Shaping Literate Minds

Developing Self-Regulated Learners

Linda J. Dorn • Carla Soffos

 Stenhouse Publishers
Portland, Maine

Stenhouse Publishers
www.stenhouse.com

Credits
Page 34: *At the Zoo* by B. Randell, J. Giles, and A.
Smith. Copyright © 1996. Reprinted by permission
of Rigby.
Page 39: *Looking Down* by A. Smith. Copyright ©
1996. Reprinted by permission of Rigby.

Library of Congress Cataloging-in-Publication Data
Dorn, Linda J.
   Shaping literate minds : developing self-regu-
   lated learners / Linda J. Dorn, Carla Soffos.
       p. cm.
   Includes bibliographical references and index.
   ISBN 1-57110-338-4
   1. Language arts (Primary)—United States. I.
   Soffos, Carla. II. Title.
   LB1529.U6 D67 2001
   372.6'0973—dc21   2001042026

Cover design by Richard Hannus, Hannus Design
Associates
Cover photographs by Carla Soffos
Figure 3.1 by Matthew Uyeda

Manufactured in the United States of America on
acid-free paper

07 06 05 04   9 8 7 6 5

This book is dedicated to the many Arkansas teachers who have shared their knowledge and experience with us.

Contents

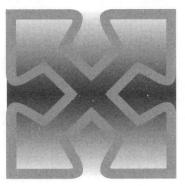

Acknowledgments

This book has been in process for the past two years. Along the way, we've worked with dedicated and talented teachers who have applied apprenticeship learning theories to their classroom practices. As the teachers worked with children, they invited us to observe and problem-solve with them on teaching and learning issues. As we wrote the chapters, we asked teachers to use the information in their literacy team meetings and provide us with feedback. Although we wrote this book, the teachers in Arkansas classrooms were with us all the way—applying theories of learning to teaching interactions with their children.

How do we find the words to thank these teachers? In this acknowledgment, we offer a small token of our deepest respect and appreciation for all their hard work and commitment to this literacy model. First, we'd like to thank the staff at Boone Park Elementary in the North Little Rock School District. Donnie Skinner is the literacy coach; Julie Dibee and Sabrina Kessler are first-grade teachers; Mavis Cherry is the principal; and Esther Crawford is the director of elementary education. In Chapter 2 you'll visit in Julie's first-grade classroom; it's an exciting place where all children are actively involved in their literacy learning. In Chapter 6 you'll read about Donnie's typical day as a literacy coach in the school, and you'll meet Sabrina, a model classroom teacher who serves as a mentor for Linda Wilsey, a novice teacher to this literacy model. Down the hallway, Julie serves as a mentor teacher for Andrea Fortner. Boone Park Elementary is a high-poverty school, where children are overcoming the challenges of poverty and achieving high literacy levels. The teachers in this school have opened their doors to visitors across Arkansas and other states, and we thank them for sharing their knowledge and experience with so many other teachers.

This same level of commitment is true for all the literacy coaches in our state. To these special teachers, we give our heartfelt thanks: Laura McKinney, Franklin Elementary, Blytheville; Sue Tilley, Greenbrier Primary; Lenett Thrasher, Greenbrier Westside; Angela Owen, Camden-Fairview Elementary; Earlena Campbell, Ivory Primary, Camden; Kim Mitchell, Green County Tech Elementary,

Paragould; Anita Bogard, Beebe Primary; Karyl Bearden, Lynch Drive, North Little Rock; Anita Smith, Seventh Street, North Little Rock; Denise Holley, Franklin Elementary, Little Rock; Sherry Chambers, Dodd Elementary, Little Rock; Tami Chandler, Crawford Elementary, Russellville; and Donna Dayer, Theodore Jones, Conway.

Also, we'd like to acknowledge the Fort Smith School District for its dedication to the Arkansas Comprehensive Literacy Model. Under the guidance of Dr. Gary Brown and Nancy Robins, the district has made a solid pledge to literacy for all children. This has resulted in a commitment to early intervention for children and high-quality professional development for teachers. We owe a special thanks to the twelve literacy coaches in the Fort Smith School District: Jamie Anne Balkman, Joan Spearman, Janie Porta, Kim Teal, Glenda Hodnett, Martha Jane Weber, Collette Haga, Sue Ann Grace, Norma Rowland, Elaine Watson, Brenda Mikel, and Wyann Stanton. These dedicated and talented teachers have made a tremendous difference in the literacy lives of teachers and children in their district. We thank you for your hard work and willingness to view challenges as opportunities to problem-solve and learn together.

We'd like to especially acknowledge our friend and colleague Teresa Treat, a first-grade teacher at Jim Stone Elementary in Conway, Arkansas. If you've viewed the video series *Organizing for Literacy*, you'll remember Teresa. Also, in the pages of this book, you'll meet Teresa and her children; she has shared with us samples of her students' work as well as videotapes of her teaching interactions. Teresa is an expert teacher, but at the same time, she is a lifelong learner—a teacher with a tentative theory that always keeps her at the cutting edge of teaching. To Teresa, we say thank you for your

willingness to share with others and to juggle your schedule to accommodate the many visitors to your classroom.

Also, we thank the seventy model classroom teachers in our state. You are indeed a very special group. We know how hard you are working to implement this literacy approach in your classrooms. We would like to express a special thanks to the teachers who've sent us videotapes and students' work. To Paula Tiffany, thank you for producing and sharing the wonderful videotape on organizing your literacy corners. To Jan Allred, Cassie Richardson, Holly Todd, Patricia Robinson, and Sherri Namors, the kindergarten and first-grade teachers at Green County Tech, thank you for sharing your children's writing samples with us. To Anita Bogard, special thanks for the videotapes of writers' workshop and student conferences.

We offer our special thanks to Krista Underwood, reading program director at the Arkansas Department of Education. Krista, a strong advocate for children and teachers, represents a beacon of light for all of us. Under her leadership, we have acquired financial and professional support to spread these literacy initiatives to Arkansas schools.

Also, we offer our heartfelt thanks to the literacy team at the University of Arkansas at Little Rock: Dr. Debbie Williams, Mike Moss, Stephanie Copes, Laurie Harrison, and Debbie Perryman. Working with this knowledgeable and dedicated group of teachers is one of the highlights of our professional career. Additionally, thank you to Cindy Franke, our secretary—yet so much more. Cindy is a teacher who contributes to our professional discussions while taking care of our business needs. To the UALR Literacy Team, we offer our heartfelt thanks for all that you've done to support the literacy efforts in our state. We can't imagine doing it without you!

In writing this book, we've shared an apprenticeship relationship with educators across our state. Together, we have problem-solved on teaching and learning issues, while shifting roles from coach to mentor, and vice versa. With the support of these talented and generous teachers, the book *Shaping Literate Minds* has finally become a reality. Furthermore, it is a teacher-certified book, tried and tested by Arkansas teachers who have used the principles and ideas with children in their own classrooms.

Last, but certainly not least, we would like to acknowledge our publishing team at Stenhouse. The principles of apprenticeship learning are clearly illustrated in the relationship between the publishing team and the authors. The staff at Stenhouse coached and mentored us throughout the writing of this new book. Without their guidance and adjustable scaffolds, the book would not have been possible. A special thanks to our friends at Stenhouse, especially Philippa Stratton, our editor. We thank Philippa for her words of encouragement, and honest and insightful feedback on our work. We thank Tom Seavey, marketing director, for his commitment and his ongoing support. Tom has worked diligently to share our apprenticeship approach with teachers and school districts across the country. Also, thanks to Martha Drury, production manager, for her talent and diligence in formatting this book to include the numerous photographs and samples of students' work. During this process, we have learned much about production challenges, and Martha was always there to work with us. And thanks to Chuck Lerch, marketing manager; Emily Field, customer service; and the many Stenhouse representatives who have promoted our work to teachers in their areas.

Also, a special thanks to the reviewers of this book: Brenda Power, Paula Moore, and Catherine Compton-Lilly, all of whom provided invaluable and thoughtful feedback. Throughout this process, the writing of this book has been a collaborative and apprenticeship project, with guidance and support from many people. We offer our heartfelt thanks to this talented and dedicated team.

Finally, we thank our families for supporting us as we've spent many long hours on this book. You have shown extraordinary patience—yet always encouraged us to move forward.

Introduction

According to Dewey (1998), the intellectual goals of education must consist of "wide-awake, careful, thorough habits of thinking" (78). These words suggest we must be reflective teachers—analytical thinkers and problem solvers. Dewey discusses the process of reflection as a self-regulated action that is guided by a personal goal. If reflective thinking is an intellectual process, how can we create opportunities in our schools to shape this process? How does teaching influence the learning process? What is the role of the curriculum? How do standards or models promote self-reflection? These questions are embedded in the pages of this book.

What is our goal in writing this book? Simply put, we have acquired a lot of experience working with children and teachers, and we want to share this information with you. Our perspectives are grounded in our daily experiences and our problem-solving interactions from the teaching field. We have tried to present numerous examples (our data) that help to make sense of the theories. And we invite you—our readers, the teachers—to further test these theoretical notions with your own students. Yet, the theories in this book are tentative: they deal with cognitive aspects of problem solving on new tasks and with the patterns of observed behavior that indicate movement to a higher plane of intellectual development. Through the wisdom and guidance of Marie Clay, we've learned to look for the external signs of knowledge and to create problem-solving interactions with children that are based on what they already know.

This is a book about problem solving—an internal tool that shapes the cognitive development of young readers and writers. At the same time, it is a book about the role of the teacher and the curriculum in structuring problem-solving opportunities. It is a book that advocates for schools to create intellectual environments that make literate thinking a top priority for children. Finally, it is a book that presents teaching and learning as collaborative processes between many people with a common goal—literacy for children.

The title of this book, *Shaping Literate Minds*, implies that intellectual development is shaped by particular circumstances. As teachers, we are critical players in promoting the intellectual development of our students. If thinking is the basis of intellectual growth, it seems that the major responsibility of the teaching profession is to create environments that engage children's minds in thinking activities. As you read this book, we encourage you to evaluate your teaching in light of children's learning development.

In Chapter 1, we discuss important theories that relate to cognitive development, specifically, the role of language in the learning process. We build the discussion around a cognitive apprenticeship model, and we provide real-life examples of teaching and learning interactions that use the principles of modeling, coaching, scaffolding, and fading. An important concept is the notion of transfer. We consider this theory a critical piece of cognitive development. In his book *How We Think* (1998), Dewey describes how learners must grasp the common elements between similar things. We relate this theory to a child who is able to talk about his knowledge but who does not apply the thinking process to a similar action. According to Dewey, "Thinking is precisely the factor that makes transfer possible and that brings it under control" (67). The theme of intellectual thinking is woven throughout this chapter and serves as the basis for the subsequent chapters.

In Chapter 2, we present a curriculum for literacy that is based on six common beliefs about reading and writing. Here we share a typical day from Julie Dibee's first-grade classroom, including schedules and specific details of the literacy program. In Chapter 3, we discuss the development of a literacy processing system with special attention to the acquisition of the print-sound code. We make the point that children acquire decoding strategies while reading continuous text and that they apply similar encoding strategies as they engage in writing activities. At the same time, through the very acts of reading and writing, the phonological and orthographic systems are strengthened. In this chapter, we provide teachers with reading and writing checklists that match levels of processing along a literacy continuum: the emergent, early, transitional, and fluent levels. To illustrate the thinking process, we share many examples of students' work, transcripts of teacher/student interactions, and pages from teachers' assessment logs. We apply the theories of processing to the practical aspects of the classroom.

In Chapter 4, we continue to build on the concept of processing, this time looking closely at the theories behind a sociocognitive spelling program. We present six beliefs that guide spelling instruction, and we share key words that provide models for teaching spelling strategies. Again, we take these theories to the practical scene of the classroom. At the first-grade level, children learn about the spelling process, specifically, how to problem-solve on words. At the second- and third-grade levels, they understand how the spelling system works, and they use a spelling workshop approach to analyze and categorize words. The shifts in instructional opportunities imply that spelling is a developmental process that changes over time. Furthermore, as students acquire greater competence (and understanding), the need for direct instruction in spelling is diminished.

In Chapter 5, we discuss the role of well-designed literacy corners in promoting independent problem-solving activity. An important point is that literacy tasks should be linked to students' reading and writing activities. In this chapter, we discuss theories of sustained attention and automaticity as goals of literacy task activities. We know from experience that literacy corners (or centers) are often used as management tools while the teacher works with small groups. We encourage teachers to view the literacy tasks from a cognitive perspective, that is, as opportunities for students to practice their knowledge and strategies in various contexts and for different purposes. We revisit the theory of building reciprocal connections between reading, writing, and spelling; we link these language processes to the literacy corner activities. Once again, we take you into real classrooms, where theory is applied to practice and teachers demonstrate how literacy task cards are introduced to students at different reading levels.

Finally, in Chapter 6, we describe an apprenticeship approach to professional development. We introduce the Arkansas Early Literacy Model, with a focus on the literacy coaching piece. We believe that school-embedded (on the job) professional development is powerful learning. In this model, teachers collaborate during the course of a normal school day. More experienced classroom teachers serve as mentors for novice teachers, and literacy coaches support teachers in implementing model classrooms that become literacy learning labs for all teachers. Literacy team meetings are a routine part of the school design, and accountability for student learning is a collaborative effort. In this chapter, we share with you specific details for implementing this model in a school setting, including a typical day in the life of Donnie Skinner, a literacy coach.

In writing this book, we want to share with you our perceptions and experiences of teaching and learning. A common theme throughout the chapters is the interrelatedness of knowledge: children develop understanding based on what they already know. We focus, also, on the development of a processing system grounded in problem solving and reflective activity. This cognitive activity is the basis of comprehension and intellectual growth. Dewey wrote, "Information is an undigested burden unless it is understood." And, in Dewey's words, "Understanding, comprehension, means that the various parts of the information are grasped in their relation to one another" (98). In this book, we share a model of learning that builds on the interconnections of literacy. From this point of view, intellectual development is shaped through the learner's ability to see and understand the relationships between reading, writing, and spelling knowledge. How does the curriculum play a role in building literacy relationships? What is the teacher's role in shaping the minds of young children? As you work with your students, we invite you to explore these questions.

Language and Learning

The teacher is a critical player in shaping the minds of young children. The teacher's theory will determine how she designs her curriculum, how she assesses her students, and how she responds to their intellectual needs. Clay (1991), in her text *Becoming Literate,* describes how teachers must hold a tentative theory—one that is open to reflection and revision as they observe children on various reading and writing tasks. From this perspective, a theory is just a tool for testing out certain beliefs as teachers apply the ideas to their ongoing observations of students' learning patterns over time and in different contexts. This notion of observing reading and writing patterns over time is critical because it provides us with a literacy context for studying the development of cognitive control as it relates to children's performance on specific literacy tasks. This means that we as teachers must hold a flexible theory—one that can be reshaped and refined according to what children are showing us as they engage in the processes of learning. As you read the various theories in this book, apply them to the children you teach. Ask questions such as, How quickly are the children learning? What are they noticing as they read? How fluent is their processing on particular tasks? Do they use their knowledge, skills, and strategies in different contexts? Simultaneously, examine your own teaching for its influence on children's learning patterns.

Learning Through Apprenticeship

Recently, educators have begun to look closely at the field of cognitive apprenticeship and its implications for classroom practice. In a report from the National Center on Education and the Economy (Rothman 1996), the significance of apprenticeship learning is explained: "Learners learn best when working beside an expert who models skilled practice and encourages and guides the learners as they create authentic products or performances for real audiences" (12).

Traditional Apprenticeship

Traditional apprenticeship has been recognized for decades as a natural way for a novice to learn a new skill under the guidance and support of a more knowledgeable person. Can you recall a time when you first learned how to ride a bicycle, bake a cake, paint a picture, or drive a car? I (Linda) can clearly remember when my mother taught me the steps for baking a cake.

I recall that my mother was an expert at baking cakes, and it seems as though I was always in the kitchen by her side, watching her. This was a social and cultural experience, a tradition that my mother and I shared together. With each cake-baking experience, she guided me gently into taking on more and more of the responsibility. She would say, "We need to make sure that we have all the ingredients. Let's check them off." Now, years later, as I look back on those sessions, it seems that my mother was always leaving an ingredient off the list, allowing me to make the discovery. "The flour!" I would exclaim. "You forgot the flour!" And my mother would comment, "How foolish of me! I forgot the flour. Now, what would a cake be like without the flour!" And we would laugh together at the thought of baking a cake without this critical ingredient. As I gained more experience with cake baking, my mother began to turn over new tasks to me. In a clear and direct manner, she would gently scaffold me to learn the specific steps on my own. Instead of doing the work for me, she would talk to me about the process: "Do you see the line here [on the measuring bowl]?" As I peered at the precise spot, my mother would explain, "We'll need to make sure that the flour comes to this line." Then I would carefully pour the flour into the measuring bowl, and my mother would lean forward with seriousness and examine the level. "You've got it!" she would exclaim. "Now pour it into the pan." Later, when the cake had baked for an appropriate amount of time, my mother would show me how to check it for

readiness. She would use explicit language to ensure that I understood the process. "Put the knife into the center of the cake, then pull it out to see if the batter is cooked all the way through." This was an exciting moment for both of us. I remember holding my breath with anticipation as I leaned forward to place the knife in exactly the right spot in the cake. If the knife came out clean, my mother would provide the appropriate feedback to confirm my work: "That's good," she would say. "Nice and clean." Through this social and cultural experience, I learned the steps involved in baking a cake. My mother, as the expert, applied all the steps of traditional apprenticeship learning. Collins, Brown, and Holum (1991) clearly describe the process: "The interplay among observation, scaffolding, and increasingly independent practice aids apprentices both in developing self-monitoring and correction skills and in integrating the skills and conceptual knowledge needed to advance toward expertise" (2).

Cognitive Apprenticeship

In traditional apprenticeship, the goal is to learn procedural steps for performing a specific task. In contrast, a cognitive apprenticeship approach goes beyond the routine steps of *what* to do on a task and emphasizes *how* to use strategies for working out task-related problems. Here, teachers provide young learners with literacy experiences that make their thinking visible (Collins, Brown, and Newman 1989). During think-aloud demonstrations, teachers model how to problem-solve on particular aspects of a reading or writing task. The process is further enhanced when teachers prompt children to apply strategies for solving problems in texts. When teachers focus attention on the thinking process, children become more conscious of their own mental actions and the significance of certain strategic behavior for solving problems. To promote this self-awareness, it is important that the literacy task be situated within an authentic context, so that the student understands the significance of the actions as they relate to solving the problem. Conceptual understanding is characterized by a student's ability to transfer knowledge, skills, and strategies over time and across changing circumstances (Lupart 1996; Bruner 1966). It is important that teachers provide students with opportunities to apply similar problem-solving actions to varied situations.

To illustrate how teachers make their thinking visible, we give an example from a writing-aloud lesson. The scene begins with Carla, the teacher, directing the children's attention to the literacy task at hand, which is to use language to describe the setting of her grandmother's farm: "Lately, we've been talking about the importance of creating interesting settings for our stories. We want our settings to be detailed enough so that our readers will be able to visualize the scene—the place where our story occurs." During this brief but focused introduction, Carla clearly states the purpose of the lesson and reminds the children that a well-designed setting is important to a story. As she continues, she creates a think-aloud context for using descriptive language: "Well, today, I want to tell you about a very special place to me—my grandmother's farm. When I was a little girl, I visited the farm every summer. As I write about the setting, I will need to use descriptive words so that you will be able to see the places in your mind's eye, just like I do." Then Carla looks off into space as though attempting to recapture the scene. She picks up her pen and begins to talk aloud as she records her message: "The road was lined with trees." She pauses momentarily and reflects aloud on her

thoughts: "Yes, I can see the sunlight as it filters through the tree branches. The light makes shadows on the road—shadows that waver from time to time as the tree branches rustle over my head and disturb their patterns." As she records the words into her story, she murmurs, "Yes, I like that description. It creates a nice, peaceful picture of the road that led to my grandmother's farm." The think-aloud process continues as Carla articulates and reflects on her own language for describing the setting of her story. At one place in her writing, she crosses out a previous line of text, speaking softly as she evaluates the quality of her words: "No, I don't like the way that sounded. I need to use a better word to describe this piece." At another point in the writing-aloud process, Carla stops and thinks about how to describe the temperature: "I'd like to talk about the way the air felt," she remarks. "That's because I want my readers to know that although it was hot outside, it didn't feel hot because of all the trees overhead." During the process, Carla demonstrates her concern for the reader as she plays around with words and considers their effect on establishing the scene. As the mini-lesson comes to an end, Carla ponders on her work: "Now, it is important that I read my writing again, because I need to listen to how I've described the scene." In this short excerpt from a writing-aloud lesson, Carla has exposed her thinking process to her students. While doing so, she has simultaneously provided them with a conceptual model that represents a well-designed setting. She has used modeling, articulating, and reflecting principles to apprentice her students in acquiring a new skill. In follow-up situations, Carla provides the children with opportunities to apply this knowledge to their own writing. At the same time, she coaches and scaffolds them in ways that will reflect their increasing control.

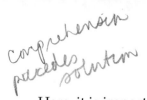
comprehension precedes solution

Elements of Apprenticeship Learning

The success of Linda's cake-baking experience and of Carla's writing-aloud lesson is characterized by four essential elements of traditional apprenticeship (Collins, Brown, and Holum 1991):

- *Modeling*. The expert provides the learner with clear models for accomplishing different parts of the task.
- *Coaching*. The expert uses language prompts and coaching techniques to keep the learner actively engaged in the task.
- *Scaffolding*. The expert provides scaffolds that are constantly adjusted to accommodate the learner's acquired skills.
- *Fading*. As the learner becomes more competent, the expert relinquishes personal responsibility for performing the task.

Modeling

Based on their observations of children's cognitive behavior during reading and writing tasks, teachers use modeling techniques, including clear demonstrations and explicit language, that advance children's learning to a higher level. In his classic book *Toward a Theory of Instruction*, Bruner (1966) describes the role of a model as a high standard to be internally achieved by the child:

> It is not so much that the teacher provides a model to imitate. Rather, it is that the teacher can become a part of the student's internal dialogue—somebody whose respect he wants, someone whose standards he wishes to make his own. It is like becoming a speaker of a language one shares with somebody. The language of that interaction becomes a part of oneself, and the standards of style and clarity that one adopts for that interaction become a part of one's own standards. (124)

Here, it is important for teachers to remember that without a conceptual model of the task, children might not understand the intention of our task-related prompts. In the writing-aloud example, Carla's model provided the students with a standard that could be used for making sense of the teacher's coaching and feedback comments at a later time. Without a model of comparison (or a benchmark example), children might not understand the goal of the instructional task, resulting in a lack of self-direction that can lead to frustration, confusion, and passivity. The ultimate goal is that children will internalize a literacy process that includes a range of good models for checking and extending their own learning.

Let's apply this principle to the introduction of a new task. For instance, before a literacy corner is opened, the teacher instructs the children in the rules that are associated with self-managing the related literacy tasks. In this example, Carla guides the children to understand the specific routines that are part of the writing corner:

Teacher: Before we open the writing corner, it is important that you understand the rules and routines for using it. You will need to know where all the materials are kept, and you will need to know the rules for using them correctly.

Then Carla walks the children through a step-by-step rehearsal for how to use the writing corner in a constructive manner. As each resource is introduced, she clearly models the process for using it, and she encourages the students to ask clarifying questions:

Teacher: Now that I've shown you how to use the dictionary, do you have any questions about this?

Nathan: What if someone else is using it and we need it?

Teacher: That's a good question. Does anyone have suggestions on what to do?

Jessica: We could begin a new story, or we could reread our story and maybe add some more to it.

In this segment, Carla activates the minds of students to reflect on self-management solutions for handling problems that might arise in the writing corner. She guides the children to consider the alternatives for negative actions. Here, she presents them with a scenario and leads them to consider the consequences of inappropriate behavior on their classmates' learning:

Teacher: Let's think about why it is so important that we return the materials to their proper places. Let's pretend that Nathan forgot to put the stapler back in its correct place on the writing table. Then Drew needs the stapler to staple his pages together. What can happen if Drew is unable to find the stapler because Nathan didn't return it to where it belonged?

Drew: I'd probably get mad.

Ricky: Yeah, and Drew might tell Mrs. Treat what Nathan did.

Caroline: But Mrs. Treat is teaching the reading group when we are working at corners. So Drew would have to interrupt the reading group.

Jessica: And that would be bad, because the kids would not get to do their reading that day.

Through these problem-solving discussions, the children are applying higher-level thinking skills. In the process, they acquire personal models (or guidelines) that enable them to deal with a range of issues. In the previous excerpt, the children are learning to think before they react, thus shaping their ability to monitor and manage their own learning behavior. A predictable environment that honors structures and rules for running the classroom helps to create independent learners.

Coaching

When children are learning a new task, teachers should use clear and precise language for directing the children's thinking to the task at hand. In contrast, excessive teacher talk can muddy the meaning and overload the child's working memory. When children participate in guided reading groups, teachers can closely observe their processing behavior and coach appropriately. In this guided reading example Teresa Treat, the teacher, uses clear, precise language that focuses the children's attention on the most efficient way for solving an immediate problem. When teachers coach children to apply flexible strategies during their reading and writing activities, children learn problem-solving processes with generative value for working out new problems.

Guided Reading Example

After the introduction to a new book, Teresa prompts the children to spread out and read the story on their own. She instructs the children to read in soft voices, so that she can listen to how they apply strategies to the text. As she listens to Mary Catherine, Teresa observes her hesitation on the word *rabbit*. She prompts Mary Catherine to think about the story: "What is Mr. Fox looking for?" Immediately, Mary Catherine responds, "Rabbit." Next, Teresa moves over to Jacob, who is reading in a word-by-word manner. Teresa prompts him for fluency: "How do you think the farmer would say that? What does the author mean when he uses big bold print?" Jacob rereads the line with expression. Now Teresa listens to Lindsey, who has just read the word *farm* for *barn*. Teresa praises her meaningful response, while prompting her to search for visual information: *"Farm* makes sense, and it sounds right. But does that word look like *farm*?" "No," says Lindsey as she self-corrects her error. Teresa continues to circulate among the readers, observing and coaching based on their individual needs. During her final round, she observes Jack as he stops at the word *shouted*. First, she prompts Jack to use meaning cues: "He's yelling at them. Do you know another word that means the same as *yelled*?" "Yes," Jack responds. *"Screamed."* Although Jack's response is meaningful, Teresa realizes that he is not checking the visual information, so she coaches him further: "Is there something about that word that you know?" Based on the final prompt, Jack looks at the word, notices the *ou* pattern, and exclaims, "Oh, it's *shouted*!"

Language prompts are used to promote thinking processes that engage children's minds in literate activity. In an earlier text (Dorn, French, and Jones 1998), we shared some examples of teacher prompts for activating children's problem-solving strategies on words and text features. The following list gives further examples of prompts that teachers can use to guide constructive and meaningful discussions about literature (Hogan and Pressley 1997; Mercer 1995):

- *Inviting elaboration.* "Can you say more about that?"
- *Admitting perplexity.* "I'm not sure what you mean. Can you explain it to me?"
- *Paraphrasing and reformulating a partially correct response.* "So you are saying that the character in the story was unhappy with the gift he received."
- *Communicating standards for explanations.* "I need to hear your evidence for predicting that the boat will sink before the rescue team arrives."
- *Refocusing the discussion.* "We all agree on that point, but let's talk more about why

you think the boy was misjudged for his crimes."
- *Prompting for refinement of language.* "When you say he went to the river, who are you referring to?"
- *Turning question back to the owner.* "I don't know. What do you think?"

Using coaching techniques, teachers can prompt children to apply knowledge, skills, and strategies from one event to another. Here's an example of how Carla coached Taylor to apply his knowledge across two literacy contexts. In the first literacy event, Carla and the children have just completed a shared reading of a familiar poem. Carla uses the poem to direct the children's attention to word patterns. Near the end of the lesson, she encourages the group to articulate the process that they would use to problem-solve on an unknown word:

Teacher: If you were writing in your journal, and you came to the word *girl,* and you couldn't remember how to write it, what would you do to help yourself?
Taylor: What I would do is try out all three chunks (*er, ir, ur*), and I'd write *girl* all three ways and try to figure out which one looks right.

Taylor can articulate a process for working on words, but the true test of his understanding will be his ability to apply the strategy in different contexts and for different purposes.

In the next literacy event, later in the day, Taylor is writing in his journal. Carla's focus for Taylor is to coach him in applying strategies for problem solving on words—specifically, strategies for checking and confirming words with similar spelling patterns. During writers' workshop, Taylor has learned a process for editing his work; that is, he circles the words that do not look right to him and tries out other spellings for solving the problem (Figure 1.1). He applies this process to the word *about,* but he neglects to use the same strategy on the word *turn* (which he has written as *trn* and has not circled as an incorrect spelling). In the following interaction, Carla coaches Taylor to apply checking and comparing strategies:

Teacher: Is that *turn*? Come up here and try it out.
Taylor: Oh, *er*!
Teacher: You said you would try it out all three ways.

With this explicit reminder, Taylor records two attempts for the word *turn* (*tirn, tern*) on his practice page. Carla realizes that she needs to increase her scaffold, so she prompts Taylor

Figure 1.1 Taylor edits his work by circling words that don't look right and trying out different spellings.

with a special cue from the poem that they had read earlier that day. "Think about *turtle,*" she says. In response, Taylor adds the word *turn* to his list. Now with all three words recorded on his practice page, Carla prompts Taylor to check the list to see which word looks right. Taylor points to an incorrect version of the word (*tirn*). Here, Carla realizes that the error will present Taylor with a productive opportunity to use a resource for further checking.

Teacher: Write it that way in your story, then look the word up in your dictionary to see if you're right.

Taylor pulls over a copy of a beginning dictionary, searches through the *T* words, and notes that the word is not in the book. "It doesn't seem to be in here," he tells Carla. With this closing remark, the instructional interaction ends, for the goal of the task—applying comparison strategies to words—has been achieved. Thus, Carla circles the correct spelling from Taylor's list of words and praises him for his problem-solving strategies. "You've learned some important ways to help yourself with your spelling. That's good work!"

During this brief interaction, the teacher has presented the child with opportunities to note relationships among various knowledge sources. We can infer that the teacher's goal is guided by her personal theory of transfer: children learn the stability of their knowledge when they attend to it in different places and for different purposes, and children learn how to apply known information to work out problems that deal with unknown information.

Scaffolding

A scaffold is a temporary support that teachers create to help children extend current skills and knowledge to a higher level of competence

(Rogoff 1990; Wood 1998). The teacher's selective intervention provides a supportive tool for the learner, thereby allowing the learner to successfully accomplish a task not otherwise possible. A scaffold is designed with just the right amount of support to enable the child to achieve the goal of the instructional task. Scaffolding closes the gap between task requirements and the skill level of the learner. As the child's competence on the task increases, the scaffold is removed, to be replaced by support at a higher level. An essential quality of a scaffold is that it be self-destructive (Cazden 1988).

It is important that we as teachers understand that scaffolding does *not* mean simplifying the task during the learning event. Instead the task remains constant while the teacher provides varying degrees of support according to how well the children are doing on the task. In the previous guided reading example, Teresa provided language scaffolds to coach individual children within a small-group setting. In the following example, the scaffolding principles (Rogoff 1990, 94) are adapted to the classroom setting. The instructional task is to teach early revision skills to first graders. Thus, the teacher selects constructive and focused examples that lead to this instructional goal. To create the appropriate learning context, the teacher has displayed a transparency copy of a student's story on the overhead screen.

Scaffolding Students in Revision Process

1. *The teacher recruits the children's interest in the task as the teacher defines it.* She introduces the task and involves the children in the goal: "Today, we'll learn how to revise a story by adding interesting details. Caroline has given us permission to put her story on the overhead screen. After Caroline reads her story, you can ask her questions about it. Then if she wants to include the information, we will work together to find the best places to insert these new details."

2. *The teacher reduces the number of steps required to solve the problem by structuring the task, so that the children can manage the components of the process and recognize when a fit with task requirements is achieved.* She keeps the interaction focused on the task of learning *how* to revise. As students ask questions and details are clarified, the teacher prompts them further: "Where do we want to include this new information in the story?" The class rereads the text and the teacher guides them to find the most appropriate place to incorporate the new details.

3. *The teacher maintains the pursuit of the goal through motivation of the children and direction of the activity.* She keeps the children involved in pursuing the goal of the activity. She praises the children for their appropriate responses and motivates them to add interesting details in revising the story.

4. *The teacher marks critical features of discrepancies between what the children have produced and the ideal solution.* When a student's suggestion for where to insert the new information is inappropriate, she guides the students to apply reflective and self-evaluative strategies: "Let's read it both ways and decide where the new information fits best in the story." She guides the students' thinking process toward the most ideal solution.

5. *The teacher controls frustration and risk in problem solving.* She uses explicit and responsive language to ensure that the students understand the task of revision. She accepts partially correct responses and promotes a problem-solving atmosphere.

6. *The teacher demonstrates an ideal version of the act to be performed.* The teacher and the children reread the finished version of the revised text. The teacher acknowledges the students' work as a good model that can be used to show others how to revise a text.

In an apprenticeship situation, structured routines provide learners with predictable and reliable scaffolds that free the mind to attend to the task at hand. For instance, Linda's cake-baking experience was characterized by predictable steps and routines that, once she had internalized them, allowed her to focus on more complex tasks. Through repeated practice, routines become associated with a particular cultural experience. In each of the previous examples, structured routines were a part of the learning experience. In the routine of guided reading groups, immediately following the book introduction the children move to their designated spots on the carpet and begin reading the story in soft voices. In the writing-aloud event, the children have acquired another routine. Here, they realize that the teacher will demonstrate a new skill for them, and they know to sit quietly so that they can observe her thinking-aloud process. In the revising lesson, the students have acquired an entirely different routine: in this literacy context, they know to ask questions and actively contribute to the revision task.

Fading

The true test of learning takes place when a student applies the knowledge, skills, and strategies gained from teacher-assisted lessons to independent work. If the child does not do this, the teacher must ask two important questions (Dorn, French, and Jones 1998):

Did I present clear and focused demonstrations for teaching a new skill?
Did I step outside the student's learning zone and move into an area of frustration?

In a well-balanced literacy program, teachers create flexible and varied opportunities for children to work at both assisted and independent levels. In whole-group assisted events, teachers will have to make compromises in their instruction, that is, teach to the instructional needs of the class majority. During small-group reading and writing events, teachers can provide students with focused instruction that is aimed at the strengths and needs of a similar population. During reading and writing conferences, teachers are able to provide intensive support that is personalized for the individual student. Through these diverse instructional settings, children receive varying degrees of teacher assistance on related types of tasks.

As you think back on the four elements of apprenticeship literacy—modeling, coaching, scaffolding, and fading—we encourage you to view them as overlapping and recursive principles. Literacy is a learned behavior that is acquired through oral and written experiences with more knowledgeable people. Literacy is not something that is transmitted to a child; it requires the active engagement of the child's mind. The skills of reading and writing are learned processes that are acquired under the guidance and support of an observant and responsive teacher. Teachers use language in ways that promote children's mental development. The four elements of apprenticeship literacy provide a natural context for connecting teaching and learning through language (Figure 1.2).

Developing Self-Regulated Learners

Studies on transfer have consistently shown that the student's self-regulation of cognitive and metacognitive strategies is the essential factor in facilitating learning and transfer (Bransford, Brown, and Cocking 1999). Transfer implies understanding—not only of *what* to do but *when* to do it (recall the writing example). So

Figure 1.2 Language is the bridge for connecting teaching and learning.

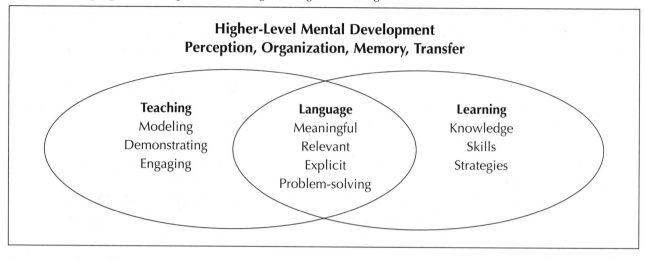

what is self-regulation? How does it relate to a student's level of understanding?

Self-regulation is grounded in Vygotsky's theory of higher-level psychological functions, such as

- Conscious awareness ("I know what I know")
- Selective attention ("I can direct my attention to what I need to attend to")
- Voluntary memory ("This is important for me to remember")

From Vygotsky's point of view, these mental processes are acquired through the use of cultural tools and symbols, specifically, artifacts that are associated with literacy acquisition. Furthermore, the development of these higher-level cognitive functions is mediated through the use of language during literacy events. Simply stated, we can characterize a self-regulated learner as one who understands how to use a range of flexible problem-solving strategies for extending learning to a higher plane. This means that self-regulation is about higher-level thinking processes.

The literature on self-regulation defines it as "the child's capacity to plan, guide, and monitor his or her behavior within and flexibly according to changing circumstances" (Diaz, Neal, and Amaya-Williams 1990, 130). What does this theory have to offer teachers? How can we use this information to help children learn how to read?

The first step in any intellectual development resides in awareness (Clay 1998). In the beginning stage, children's literacy awareness can occur vicariously in social situations with a more knowledgeable person (Bruner 1990). For instance, in Barbara Culpepper's kindergarten classroom, her students first became aware of the role of the exclamation mark during the shared reading experience. They participated by reading these punctuated parts of the story with excitement and expression. The children's awareness level was further enhanced by Barbara's comment, "When we see this mark, we've got to read it with excitement." During these social experiences, the children began to attend more closely to the form and function of the exclamation mark. Barbara described this developmental stage in their perceptual aware-

Figure 1.3 A continuum of learning control.

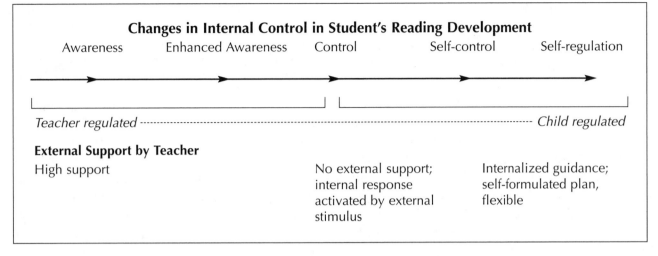

ness as a period of "being glued to the exclamation point." When the novelty of the sign wears off, the children will enter another period of control, where their reading attention is diverted to something new, and they might not notice the exclamation mark until Barbara prompts them to "read this part with excitement." Here, it is important to recognize that, although this behavior might appear to be regressive, it is actually a sign of literacy progress. This temporary diversion from what they know can occur because the children are learning how to orchestrate a range of literacy actions; thus their attention will fluctuate according to the immediate demands of the task. Through coaching, scaffolding, and repeated practice, the teacher will guide the children toward achieving higher levels of understanding. This means that a child's knowledge will ultimately become embedded into a larger network of subroutines and strategies. For instance, with Barbara's children, we can expect to see literacy development occur along a continuum of control that will result in an internalized understanding for the exclamation mark. When this happens, the printed sign

will automatically trigger the child's fluent and expressive reading.

Figure 1.3 shows how a continuum of learning control might look as a learner moves toward self-regulation. First, the child must become aware of a concept before any intellectual movement can proceed. Here, it is up to the teacher to structure the learning event so that children's perceptual processes are awakened and they begin to notice new detail. The next level of awareness occurs when a child becomes more conscious of the item. When a child acquires this heightened level of awareness, the teacher transfers some responsibility for the learning task and simultaneously structures opportunities for the child to discover the information on his own. Next, at the level of control, the child shows the capacity to use his knowledge on more complex tasks; thus the teacher begins to hold the child more accountable for his actions. Even so, at this level, the child will still require support from the teacher, generally in the form of vague reminders to apply a known skill or strategy to a particular task. For instance, during reading, if a child makes an error on a known word or neglects to use a familiar strategy, the teacher might prompt the child by saying, "What can you do to help yourself?" The important point here is that the child did not apply the strategy on his own. This level of control is characterized by a stimulus-response pattern, where the teacher's prompt represents the stimulus that activates the child's response to the problem at hand. As the child gains more experience and successful practice on the task, he internalizes the teacher's language as his own inner voice that he uses to tell himself what to do. At the level of self-control, the child will often talk himself through a problem. For example, he might reflect, "No, that doesn't look right" or comment on his own knowledge: "I see my name inside that word!" At the highest level, that of self-regulation, the child's behavior is represented as a flexible network of well-orchestrated and internalized actions. Here, the child exhibits the ability to use his knowledge for monitoring, planning, and extending his own learning. The self-regulated learner has developed a personal management system for advancing learning to higher intellectual levels.

Earlier, we asked, Why is this theory important to teachers of young children? First, the role of the teacher for guiding children's thinking to higher levels of cognitive control is critical. Teachers must be good observers of children's literacy behavior and be able to structure learning opportunities with adjustable and self-destructing scaffolds that support children's movement to higher levels of mental development. Furthermore, teachers must understand that a child's regressive behavior does not necessarily mean that the child has a learning problem; rather, they should view this momentary relapse as an opportunity to help young children learn *how* to consolidate multiple sources of information. Through scaffolding, articulating, and coach-

ing techniques, teachers play a vital role in shaping the literate minds of young children.

The Co-Construction of Meaning

The goal of any interaction is to construct meaning. We define meaning as a personal state of mind, a mental process that occurs as an individual strives to build connections between the current experience and its relationship to other relevant memories. The meaning-making experience shares an association with all kinds of related memories. For instance, one memorable event can be triggered by a certain smell, a particular sound, or even a feeling that makes us think about the event. These associated memories are part of a larger network of semantic experiences that all work together to shape our personal interpretations of life. Simply put, higher-level understanding occurs when a learner realizes the significance of her mental resources for seeing relationships, building connections, and acquiring new knowledge. In *Classroom Discourse*, Cazden (1988) emphasizes the role of the teacher in the meaning-making process:

> In order to learn, students must use what they already know so as to give meaning to what the teacher presents to them. Speech makes available to reflection the processes by which they relate new knowledge to old. But this possibility depends on the social relationships, the communication system, which the teacher sets up. (Douglas Barnes, as quoted by Cazden, 2)

For teachers, it is important to recognize that a child's perspective on literacy will be influenced by what she already knows. In shaping the literate mind, teachers must strive to find the meaningfulness in children's personal perspectives and thus create opportunities for children to learn *how* to build pathways between what they already know and the more conventional definitions. If a child does not understand the intention of the teacher's language, it is the teacher's responsibility to make adjustments in her language to accommodate the child's understanding. When understanding occurs, meaning becomes a shared experience. The achievement of shared meaning is described as intersubjectivity (Wertsch 1985).

The following examples illustrate the concept of intersubjectivity as it relates to the teacher/student interaction that takes place around shared literacy experiences. The teacher is Liz Jorgenson, a student of Linda's at the university, and the child is Timothy, one of her first-grade students. The transcripts are based on a study that Liz conducted on ways that language is used between teachers and students as they strive to create intersubjectivity (Jorgenson 1999).

In the first event, Liz and Timothy are conversing about a story that they have just read. The story is about a swarm of bees that chase a giant through the town. The conversation begins with Timothy's telling Liz about the time when six bees chased him. "How did you get away?" Liz inquires. Timothy explains, "It's because I didn't open my mouth. When you run, if you keep your mouth closed, you can run faster." Then, Liz prompts further, "What would have happened if you had had your mouth open?" Timothy responds, "I would have stopped, and they [the bees] would have stung me." Timothy's explanation is based on a personal perspective; nevertheless, his comment illustrates a logical interpretation for cause-and-effect relationships.

Findings from Liz's study indicate that the co-construction of meaning is a natural force that drives the conversation between individuals. When meaning breaks down, the negotiating process to reestablish meaning is an automatic reaction for both participants. Liz describes how the natural drive for meaning making is so embedded in the conversational exchange that the teacher and child may not even realize they're negotiating for understanding. In the process of negotiating for meaning, children are acquiring new understandings about literacy. For example, during a writing conference, Timothy shares details of a visit from his cousin, Little Harvey, who was often naughty. Following Timothy's humorous story about the antics of Little Harvey, Liz asked, "Is Little Harvey a brat?" With seriousness, Timothy responded, "No, he's a Randolph." Although Timothy's definition for *brat* is not the same as Liz's definition, the semantic quality of the conversation is not jeopardized by his lack of understanding.

On the other hand, Liz observed, "The need for intersubjectivity may be such that conversation stops and spins its wheels until it can be reestablished" (Jorgenson 1999, 32). The conversation in the next example took place shortly after Timothy had just received his new glasses. Previously, Timothy had struggled with writing his stories, but on this particular day he composes and writes a new story with confidence and ease. As he shares the story with Liz, the conversation takes an interesting turn: "Wow, that was fast!" Timothy remarks at the end of his story. "Yes," Liz responds. "You did write particularly fast today." Timothy comments, "I think it's because of my glasses." At this point, Liz looks puzzled, for she is thinking about Timothy's writing accomplishments from a literacy perspective, that is, Timothy is becoming a better writer with practice. Timothy, however, is thinking about his writing performance from a different perspective: today his perspective is personally influenced by his ability to see more clearly. Both Timothy and Liz are having difficulty seeing the other person's perspective, and the quest for meaning becomes stronger as Liz guides

Timothy to explain his comments. "Why do you think your glasses helped you write faster?" Liz inquires. Timothy explains, "They've got medicine in them." Now Liz is really puzzled, and she continues to seek the meaning in Timothy's comment. "How do you know they've got medicine in them?" "Because the doctor told me." With this comment, Liz suddenly understands: "Oh, you mean a prescription! Your glasses have a prescription and that helps you to see better. And that is helping you to write faster, too." Here, intersubjectivity was achieved because the need to understand was a driving force that guided the semantic direction of the conversation.

From Vygotsky's (1978) point of view, language is a tool for shaping higher-level understanding. Vygotksy describes how intellectual development occurs as children work in two complementary learning zones:

- *Zone of actual development (ZAD).* This is where a child can accomplish a learning task independently. The ZAD is characterized as a child's independent level of knowledge.
- *Zone of Proximal Development (ZPD).* This is where the child is able to accomplish a task but requires the assistance and guidance of a more knowledgeable person. The ZPD is the area of a child's potential development, but success in this area depends on the teacher's ability to structure appropriate tasks and use language to guide the child's understanding to a higher level.

Here is an important point for teachers to think about: *If a child is working in his zone of proximal development, the teacher will expect to see a discrepancy between the teacher's definition and the child's interpretation of the task.* A different viewpoint can be expected, simply because the teacher is the more experienced and knowledgeable person on this particular task.

Thinking by Analogy

During meaningful discussions with a more literate person, children acquire a new understanding about literacy. In the process, they learn how to revise their original thinking to match more conventional models. This leads us to our final discussion in this chapter—thinking by analogy. Eisner (1998) states,

> Since no teacher has direct access to a child's mind, it is the child's ability to see the connections between the example the teacher uses, what the child already knows, and what the teacher hopes he or she will understand that makes the example instrumental to new meaning. In short, understanding depends on the child's ability to think by analogy, and to grasp, often through metaphor, what needs to be understood. (79)

What does this theory have to offer to teachers? How does it relate to shaping the literate minds of children? First, let's examine what we mean by "thinking by analogy." The definition of an analogy implies that two or more sources of information are being compared with each other. For teachers, this means that a child must apply strategies of comparison that use the known source of information as a model to compare with the unknown source of information. How are the sources the same? How are they different? Without a model, the child has no exemplar for learning how to think by analogy. In other words, without a model for comparison, the mind is forced to rely on the memorization of abstract information, which is a lower-level thinking process. In contrast, the ability to think by analogy is characteristic of higher-level thinking strategies and is directly related to the development of self-regulated learning.

Teachers must provide children with problem-solving opportunities to learn how to think by analogy. Literacy events must be structured in such a way that children have available models for comparing multiple sources of information. Two kinds of models that work together to help children learn how to compare and analyze information are the following:

- *Internal model.* This is the child's mental representation for the concept—his own knowledge. It is critical that the child recognize the potential of his knowledge for comparing and analyzing unknown information. The goal is that the child will realize, "This is what I know, and I can use my own knowledge to help me learn something new."

- *External model.* This is the teacher's example for demonstrating the concept to be learned. Although the teacher provides the external model, the child must be able to use his internal experience to make sense of the teacher's model. If the child does not have the appropriate background experience, the teacher's model can be an abstract concept for the child. The goal here is that the child will realize, "This is how it should look, and I can use what I already know to help me reach the goal."

When teachers prompt children to apply problem-solving strategies as they read, they provide them with a means for learning how to think by analogy. For instance, a prompt such as, "Think of what would make sense and look right," provides the child with a context for learning how to integrate multiple sources of information within text. However, if the child does not understand the significance of the teacher's prompt as it relates to his problem-

solving actions, higher-level thinking will *not* occur. In order for teachers to make good decisions about the child's processing actions, they should ask

What source of information did the child use in making the error?

What source of information did the child neglect in making the error?

How do I prompt the child in such a way that he learns how to integrate multiple sources of information?

Here is an example that illustrates how the teacher must scaffold the learning process so that the child acquires successful practice with integrating information. For instance, when a child is learning how to read, the child has limited print knowledge to bring to the integration process, so the teacher must accept responsibility for filling in the literacy gaps. Therefore, when the child makes an error and the teacher prompts the child to check his work, he will have a model for comparing what he just said with what he should have said (as represented by the printed word). Now, think for a moment about the mental activity that occurs when a child is prompted to compare two responses—in this case, his oral structure to the text structure. Say that the child is reading and makes an error that reflects a structural miscue (which is based on his oral language pattern). The teacher asks a standard prompt that is frequently used by teachers to promote a child's attention to structural cues: "Does that sound right [what you just said]?" (Figure 1.4). In order for higher-level thinking to occur, the child must understand the significance of the teacher's prompt, and he must possess adequate models for comparing three language sources:

- *Pronoun model.* The child must ask himself what the pronoun *that* represents in the

Figure 1.4 Learning how to think in analogy.

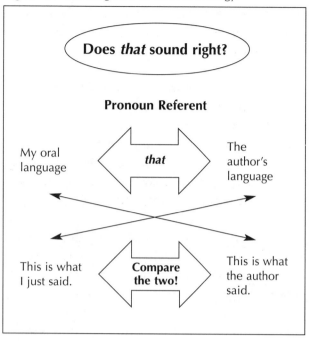

Figure 1.5 Learning how to think in analogy.

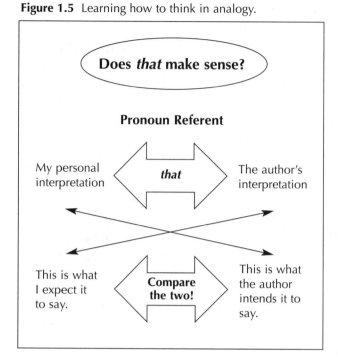

prompt "Does *that* sound right?" In this case, the pronoun stands for the child's oral language response, in other words, the miscue that he just substituted on the page.

- *Oral language model.* This is the easiest model for the child because it is grounded in his control of oral language. This personal model will then represent a comparison example for checking against the text structure.

- *Text language model.* This is the model for book language. In order for the child to compare how his oral structure relates to the book structure, he will need to have some experience with the language of the book. How does the emergent reader acquire the book model? Again, the role of the teacher is the critical factor, for the teacher provides the child with a book introduction that includes exposure to the language structures and specialized vocabulary.

We could apply this same principle to any of the language prompts that teachers use with children. Consider again the demands on the mind when a child is asked a simple question such as, "Does *that* make sense?" (Figure 1.5). As we said about intersubjectivity, the meaning-making process is directly influenced by the individual's personal perspective, which in this case can interfere with taking on the author's perspective. If the child does not have the necessary background for cross-referencing the various sources of information (the pronoun referent, the child's interpretation, the author's intention), the child may not learn the connection between the teacher's prompt and his internal process for checking. The value of these prompts is not in the question itself but in the teacher's ability to know *when* to ask the appropriate question for stimulating the child's problem-solving activity. Simultaneously, the teacher must realize the complexity of the problem-solving process as it relates to comparing

*prompting for v±
they can answer but
do they understand?*

and analyzing multiple sources of information. The teacher must provide the necessary background (e.g., through book introductions and literature discussions) that will provide the child with a tool for thinking by analogy. Through successful experiences, children become aware of the significance of the teacher's language and their problem-solving actions. Cazden (1988) describes the difference in answering versus understanding: "There is a critical difference between helping a child somehow get a particular answer and helping a child gain a conceptual understanding from which answers to similar questions can be constructed at a future time."

Generative learning

Subsequent chapters discuss applying the theory of analogy to the classroom and include specific examples from spelling lessons, word-building activities, mini-lessons during writers' workshop, and guided reading lessons. In summary, here are some underlying principles that relate to the concept of thinking by analogy:

- Multiple sources of information are compared and analyzed according to their similarities and differences.
- Known information represents a model for comparison.
- Strategies are used to note relationships and patterns.
- Thinking by analogy requires higher-level thinking processes.

How can language promote transfer?

Closing Thoughts

In recent years, the literacy needs of our society have changed dramatically. The demands on the literate mind are very different today than they were fifty years ago. During the 1950s, the major responsibility of educational training was to ensure that people had a repertoire of basic information that was culturally associated with being well-rounded and literate. A per-

son had to learn a lot of facts because at that time if one wanted to know something, one had to search one's memories for the information (too often, it had already been forgotten). In our present technological society, the demands on the mind are much different, for if one wants to know about a topic, one can go to the Internet and within minutes have more information than can possibly be used. Now the challenge for the mind is not so much *what* can be remembered but *how* to access information and apply it toward learning new information. In other words, the mind must know *how* to select relevant facts, see patterns within related areas, and organize knowledge to meet specific learning goals. Learning is meaningful, purposeful, self-directed, and generative, for it leads to new discoveries and new knowledge.

With these thoughts in mind, we share a reference from the field of business. Recently, a group of educators asked the manager of a successful business, "What type of employee would you hire in your business?" His response was immediate and confident: "I want an employee with an inquiring mind—one who knows how to recognize problems and seek creative solutions." As teachers, we have the responsibility to provide a "thinking" curriculum that actively engages the minds of children in problem-solving situations, thus preparing them for the challenges of tomorrow.

In this chapter, we have emphasized the reciprocal relationship between teaching and learning. From a cognitive apprenticeship approach, the teacher is the critical player in shaping children's literate minds. In subsequent chapters, we apply these learning theories to the everyday practical situations of primary classrooms. Here are some thoughts to take with you: How is today's curriculum influencing tomorrow's learning? Are children acquiring strategies today that will enable them to problem-solve tomorrow?

A Curriculum for Literacy

On the road to literacy, children take individual paths that are influenced by their prior experiences and their personal perceptions of the world. The goal of the curriculum is to ensure that all children, regardless of where they are on the path to literacy, are provided with appropriate opportunities for reaching their highest potential. Here, we must recognize that some children will enter the classroom behind their peers, whereas others will enter the classroom with advanced skills and knowledge. Yet a third group of children will fit right into the school's definition for where students should be achieving according to grade-level expectations. Traditionally, the classroom curriculum has been designed for this average-performing group of students. Instructional models such as whole-group reading (where all children are reading in the same basal text at the same time) teach to the middle group, that is, those children who fit into the school's literacy classification for a grade-level student. In too many cases, a one-size-fits-all curriculum has been applied to the primary class, thus ignoring the diverse strengths and needs of a typical classroom culture.

The teacher must ensure that all children—from the lowest-performing to the highest-performing—will receive appropriate literacy experiences that will enable them to reach their highest potential in literacy. This means that teachers must first determine where young children are along a literacy continuum and then design a literacy curriculum that is based on their strengths and needs. Teachers must be knowledgeable about the literacy process, specifically, the developmental changes that occur in reading and writing as the child moves to a higher level of competency. This implies that assessment and instruction share a reciprocal relationship: teachers must assess the quality of their teaching as it relates to children's learning.

In the next two chapters, we explore the link between the literacy curriculum, high-quality literacy standards, and children's literacy development. How does a teacher design a literacy program that enables young children to achieve high standards in reading and writing literacy? What are reading and writing benchmarks that provide teachers with ways of assessing how well children are learning along a literacy continuum? How can teachers measure change over time as children become more efficient readers and writers? These questions give us a focal point for discussing how the curriculum can become a model for promoting literacy in the primary grades.

Common Beliefs About Literacy Development

Although reading experts might disagree on specific details of teaching reading, they share some common beliefs about young children's literacy development. Here are some important learning principles that support a primary curriculum for literacy:

1. *Children become better readers and writers with practice.* When students read a lot, they become more efficient readers. The same holds true for the writing process: as students engage in meaningful writing experiences, they become better writers. In contrast, if children have limited opportunities to read and write in their classrooms, they are deprived of the very experiences that move their literacy development forward. A primary classroom should provide many opportunities for children to practice successful reading and writing behavior (New Standards Primary Committee 1999, 23).

Read, Read, and Read Still More

- *Kindergarten.* Read or reread—independently or with another student or adult—two to four familiar books each day. Listen to one or two books read aloud each day at school and at home.
- *First grade.* Read—independently or with assistance—four or more books each day. Hear two to four books or other texts read aloud each day.
- *Second grade.* Read one or two short books or long chapters each day. Listen to and discuss each day one text that is longer and more difficult than what can be read independently.
- *Third grade.* Read 30 chapter books per year. Listen to and discuss at least one chapter read aloud each day.

New Standards Primary Committee (1999, 23)

2. *Reading and writing are reciprocal processes.* The very acts of reading and writing require that children apply perceptual and cognitive strategies, both of which share common relationships for working with written language. When children become more competent in one area, similar advances in the other area will be observed.

3. *Children's past experiences form a knowledge base for new learning.* All new learning is grounded in old learning. Children's prior knowledge enables them to make sense of new learning situations. They build connections and establish relationships between what they already know and what they need to know. Therefore, teachers must be good observers of children's literacy behavior and provide them with opportunities to use their current knowledge for learning new information.

4. *Beginning readers should have many opportunities to learn about print.* Through meaningful experiences with a more literate person, children acquire important information about the printed word. During literacy activities, children learn how to attend to print. They begin to notice letter and word features, and they learn book concepts. They learn to use pictures and story patterns to make text predictions. They play with the language of books, and they begin to use phrases and vocabulary from their favorite books in their everyday language. Through these literacy experiences, children acquire a foundation that scaffolds their reading development.

5. *Hearing books read aloud is a vital part of learning how to read.* During read-aloud events, young children are exposed to literature that is

at a higher level than their independent reading level. Simultaneously, they hear fluent and expressive reading that represents a standard for how reading should sound. They learn to listen to clues in the story that signal important events; and they acquire an understanding for how stories work, including text features for particular genre, authors' techniques, and specialized vocabulary.

6. *Children should engage in active book discussions and share their reading and writing with others.* During book conversations, children learn how to use language to talk about written texts. They learn how to listen to different viewpoints and to present evidence that supports their own perspectives. They strengthen their knowledge of stories as they apply comprehension skills to texts, such as summarizing, comparing, reflecting, and linking strategies. In these situations, children learn to value the language of literacy—talking about books, reading stories to each other, and sharing their own writing with classmates.

7. *Reading is a meaning-making, problem-solving process.* When children read, they apply a range of problem-solving strategies that are guided by their desire to gain meaning from the text. Good readers make fast decisions that are based on the smooth integration of visual, syntactic, and semantic cues from the text. They apply strategies of comprehension that include monitoring, searching, comparing, and self-correcting actions. They acquire accuracy of words and meanings as they problem-solve on texts of graded difficulty (Fountas and Pinnell 1996). Through successful problem-solving opportunities, children learn how to orchestrate a range of elements (visual information, concept knowledge, language patterns, meaning cues, text structures, background experience) into a fluent translation of the author's message (Clay 1991). This implies that young readers must have opportunities to

practice the orchestration process on texts that contain rich cue sources. Furthermore, teachers must understand how students are using (or neglecting) the textual cues, thus prompting them to cue integration.

Definitions of Word Recognition, Integration, and Orchestration

Word recognition is a lower-level process that is characterized by the reader's ability to recognize the word in the absence of other cues sources. Here, readers are able to direct their full attention to the identification process as determined by the graphophonemic cues. In the early stages of reading, many students can identify words in isolation but may have difficulty with reading or writing the same word as it occurs within texts.

Integration relates to the reader's ability to unite the three sources of textual information (the story meaning, the structural cues of language, and the visual patterns of print) into a coherent reading that represents the author's intended message. Cue integration is more complex than reading an isolated word, as it involves the cross-referencing of multiple sources of textual information.

Orchestration represents a higher level of cognitive organization. Here, other sources of nonvisual information (e.g., problem-solving strategies, background experience, content knowledge, motivational and emotional effects) may influence how well the reader is able to integrate the textual sources. In the early stages of reading, a child can exhibit regressive behavior (e.g., misreading or hesitating on a known word) that indicates the interference of other information. The goal of reading is the smooth orchestration of all information (both visual and nonvisual) in a meaningful transaction with the text.

Teaching for the Orchestration Process

Donnie Skinner, a first-grade teacher, has just introduced a new book entitled *Mushrooms for*

Dinner (Randell 1994) to a guided reading group of early readers. When one student, Shanna, encounters the phrase "ring of mushrooms," she hesitates on the word *ring*. She articulates the *r* and the *ing* parts of the word, but when she blends them back together, she looks puzzled. Here, in context, Shanna is faced with the challenge of checking a familiar word within an unexpected language phrase. Her ability to orchestrate this process represents the highest level of word knowledge. Successful readers must be able to integrate multiple sources for gaining the precise meaning for a particular text. This means that beginning readers must be provided with guided opportunities to use their knowledge in flexible ways to resolve problems. In Shanna's case, Donnie validates her word-solving attempt. "You know that word is *ring* because you broke it apart when you were reading it." Next, she prompts her to integrate this information with the meaning and language sources. She explains, "But it didn't sound right to you in this sentence, did it?" Then Donnie engages Shanna in a brief discussion about the meaning of the phrase "ring of mushrooms." Finally, she prompts Shanna to put it all together: "Now, read it again and think of what would make sense *and* look right." When teachers look for opportunities that promote an orchestration process, children can practice their word knowledge in flexible ways that result in accurate, meaningful reading.

8. *Beginning readers should have a well-designed phonics program.* In the primary grades, children should have a well-designed phonics program that promotes knowledge of letters, sounds, words, and phonological units. In kindergarten, students should develop awareness for the sounds of language (phonological awareness), and they should acquire some letter-sound knowledge. In first grade, they should refine their knowledge of letters and sounds, acquire a solid core of high-frequency words, and learn strategies for analyzing words according to their spelling patterns. Furthermore, children should have ample opportunities to practice their phonological skills while reading texts that reflect a gradient of difficulty. At the same time, children should have daily practice in applying word-solving strategies to their own writing.

9. *Children should write every day.* In meaningful interactions with a more knowledgeable person, children develop an understanding for the writing process. As they strive to create a balance between composing and transcribing a written text, they acquire important skills for orchestrating their writing knowledge. They learn the functional purposes of different types of writing; they learn how to problem-solve on words and use resources for checking; they learn how to put ideas into sentences and find the best words to express their thoughts. During daily writing opportunities, young children learn how to revise and edit their messages for a public audience (Figure 2.1). Writing provides children with a way of consolidating their knowledge about print at four language levels: ideas, sentences, words, and letters.

Figure 2.1 Kim Mitchell's writing wall. Children's work demonstrates an understanding of the writing process.

These common beliefs provide teachers with a framework for designing a curriculum for literacy. What types of literacy events would be included in a primary classroom? If the preceding theories are vital for literacy development, we must examine our curriculum for evidence of these elements.

A Curriculum for Literacy

In Julie Dibee's first-grade classroom, she realizes the importance of daily reading. She knows that her children's reading development is shaped by their successful reading practice. The goal is that her first graders will read about 100 to 150 books during the school year. In her classroom, Julie has created a literacy culture, where children perceive reading and writing as a natural part of their daily lives. Here, reading is a routine practice that begins as soon as the children enter the classroom. Figure 2.2 shows Julie's schedule for literacy in her classroom.

Julie's classroom is typical: she has some children who are reading books at kindergarten levels, other children who are reading at typical first-grade levels, and a smaller proportion of children who are reading from chapter books that are suitable for second- and third-grade students. Julie realizes that although the children are at different places in their reading development, each child will achieve reading success in time, with some children taking a little longer and requiring more assistance than other children. She has organized the first part of the day to include an independent reading period so that all children can practice successful reading habits. During this twenty-minute block of time, Julie circulates among the children, takes a running record on two or three children each morning, and interacts with them according to their personal strengths and needs. She carries a small observation reading log with her, where she records brief notes about the children's independent reading behavior (see Chapter 3 for details on observation logs).

Next, Julie pulls her class together for a group meeting, which begins with a shared reading experience. Here, she guides the children to apply strategies through group problem-solving discussions. She validates the diversity within the group as she provides opportunities for everyone to actively participate in the story event. Julie often includes plays with individual and group parts assigned to the children. She believes that this genre promotes special attention to expressive reading and character development, both of which play an important role in comprehension. Frequently, Julie uses poetry during this time because the natural structure of poetry provides her students with a rich backdrop for learning about language. She knows that her first graders must learn how to coordinate sound units with spelling patterns, and she looks for opportunities in text that help to promote the children's phonological knowledge. During shared reading, Julie plans for a range of guided experiences that promote children's problem-solving strategies at both the text and word levels. She uses flexible language prompts to accommodate the strengths and needs of the individual children within the larger group. Today, for instance, she engages the emergent readers in a discussion about letter-sound relationships. She is aware that at the emergent stage of reading (see Chapter 3), the children need to make links between letter-to-sound analysis during reading and sound-to-letter analysis during writing. Julie believes that the shared reading context will provide the children with an instructional opportunity for acquiring this important skill. Thus, she uses explicit language to direct their attention

Figure 2.2 First-Grade Literacy Schedule

8:00–8:20	***Independent Reading:*** Students practice fluency and strategies on familiar or easy texts. Use this time to take running records on two or three students for continuing assessment. Have students get book boxes and read at their desks.
8:20–8:40	***Shared Reading:*** Poetry transparencies, Big Books, poems, cut-up poems, ABC chart, songs, plays, etc. Teacher engages children in whole-group shared experience that focuses on print conventions and strategies.
8:40–9:10	***Spelling/Phonics:*** This time is used to work on learning strategies for solving words, e.g., building up and breaking apart known words, adding endings, letter-sound matches, onset and rime patterns. The spelling words are placed in the literacy corner for practice.
9:10–9:15	***Literacy Corner Assignments:*** Teacher explains literacy corner rotations.
9:15–10:45	***Guided Reading and Assisted Writing Small Groups:*** Students attend small groups at their instructional level. During this block of time, other students are working in literacy corners (word building, writing, math, science, listening, language, ABC, name, rhythm and rhyme, and reading).
10:45–11:00	***Recess***
11:00–11:30	***Lunch***
11:30–11:50	***Read-Aloud:*** Teacher reads aloud to students. The read-aloud can be related to mini-lessons in reading/writing or to content-area studies.
11:50–12:30	***Activity Time*** M—Computer T—Enrichment W—P.E. TH—Music F—Library
12:30–1:15	***Writers' Workshop:*** Whole-group mini-lessons focus on areas of organization, processes, skills, strategies, and craft (10 minutes). Students write independently and teacher conducts five to seven teacher-scheduled conferences and one to two student-scheduled conferences each day. Peer conferences and small-group conferences are held as needed. (See sign-up schedule on wall.) Published work is shared in author's chair.
1:15–1:30	***Recess***
1:30–2:30	***Math:*** Plan whole-group lessons that focus on computation and problem-solving strategies. Provide independent practice and work with students who need extra in specific areas.
2:30–3:00	***Other: Social Studies or Science:*** Use informational books from guided reading sets and Big Books to engage the group. Also, incorporate hands-on activities, experiments, and writing activities into this block.
3:00–3:20	***Car riders dismissed at 3:00. Bus riders dismissed at 3:10 to 3:15.***
3:30–4:30	***Literacy Team Meetings on Tuesday Each Week:*** Bring student writing folders. Plan to change guided reading groups on assessment wall.

to the process: "What letter would you expect to see at the beginning of *went*?" Quickly, the children identify the letter that makes the *w* sound and locate the word in the text. Then Julie prompts the children to think of other words that begin with the same letter, and she records a few examples on a chart tablet. With her closing comment, Julie reminds the children of the reading and writing connection: "When you are writing a story, you can use these words to help you with other words that start with the same sound." As soon as the children begin to attend to letter-sound relationships, Julie will direct their attention to larger patterns within language. Here, she will continue to look for opportunities to help the children become more flexible with their letter-sound knowledge.

Prompting Children for Letter Patterns During Shared Reading

Teacher/Student Interaction	Analysis
T: (*Records the word* sister *on the chart tablet.*) What is this word?	Presents visual information; prompts for letter-sound analysis
S: *Sister!*	Attends and searches text
T: Can you find other words that end like *sister*?	Prompts for letter-sound analysis
S: *Bigger! Brother!*	Attends and searches text
T: (*Records the two new words under* sister.) What is the same about these words?	Presents comparison model; prompts for visual analysis
S: They all end with *er!*	Attends and searches text
T: (*Underlines the* er *part on all three words; writes the* er *pattern at the top of the chart.*) Do you know other words that end with the same sound?	Confirms visual pattern; classifies visual pattern; prompts for sound-letter analysis from oral language
S: *Other! Father! Over! River!*	Attends, searches memory (sound-letter analysis)
T: (*Records the words under the* er *pattern.*) Can you see the part of the word that looks the same? Do they sound alike? Do they look alike?	Presents visual model; prompts for visual analysis; prompts for sound analysis

---

Immediately following the shared reading, Julie involves the group in a constructive spelling lesson that focuses on learning how words work. Throughout the year, she has guided the children to acquire word knowledge through explicit teaching opportunities, for example, direct sound-to-letter match in one-syllable words, serial order in word patterns, and constructing high-frequency words (see Chapter 4 on spelling instruction). Today, Julie builds on the children's prior experiences with spelling patterns, specifically, patterns that they had discussed earlier from the poetry event. She believes that the children must learn analytical ways to problem-solve on words, and she realizes the importance of comparison strategies. Here, she guides the children to observe how two spelling patterns can be represented by one sound; then she engages the class in generating new words that fit the pattern. As the children provide examples, Julie records the words on a chart, which she later displays on the classroom wall. She encourages the children to apply this principle to their independent work in the word-building corner. Also, Julie will look for other opportunities during the students' reading and writing activities to highlight this knowledge.

As the group meeting ends, the children know the routine for the next ninety-minute literacy block. Here, Julie realizes that she will need to provide different levels of assistance to meet the diverse needs of her students. Today, she plans to meet with two guided reading groups and one literature discussion group (Figure 2.3). Although she plans to meet with each group for twenty to thirty minutes, Julie remains tentative, because she knows that the amount of time for each group will need to be adjusted to match the students' needs. She is also aware that the children will learn at different paces; therefore, her groups must remain flexible and change according to how well

Figure 2.3 Julie Dibee's small-group schedule.

Day	Group 1	Group 2	Group 3	Extra
Monday	Guided reading and book talk (Early Group)	Guided reading and book talk (Transitional Group)	Literature discussion group (Fluent Group); after group gets started they can read silently.	Check on independent work in literacy corners
Tuesday	Interactive writing and independent writing (Early Group)	Writing aloud and independent writing (Transitional Group)	Silent reading and individual reading; conferences with teacher	Guided reading and book talk (Early Group)
Wednesday	Guided reading and book talk (Early Group)	Guided reading and book talk (Transitional Group)	Peer conferences and prepare literature extension activity	
Thursday	Interactive writing and independent writing (Early Group)	Guided reading and book talk (Transitional Group)	Literature discussion with teacher and group members	Check on independent work in literacy corners
Friday	Guided reading and book talk (Early Group)	Guided reading and book talk (Transitional Group)	Sharing of literature extension activities	Check on independent work in literacy corners

individual students are progressing. Julie understands that small-group assisted reading lessons will provide her students with productive opportunities to apply problem-solving strategies in books that are geared to their instructional reading levels.

Once or twice weekly, during this ninety-minute literacy block, Julie will conduct small-group assisted writing lessons for students who need extra help in specific areas. Julie is well aware of the reciprocal relationship between reading and writing, and she realizes that her students must learn how to build connections between their reading and writing knowledge. Within her classroom, the diversity in writing is even wider than the diversity in reading. For instance, the children who are reading in chapter books are also producing written texts that span over several days. Other

children are struggling with simple sentences that describe a picture. Julie understands that writing is a critical piece of literacy development and that small-group writing lessons will allow her to scaffold each student at his or her own level of understanding.

During this same literacy block, Julie ensures that the other children are working constructively in literacy corners. Here, the children practice their literacy knowledge and skills on reading and writing tasks that are specially designed to promote flexibility and automaticity. Julie knows that children must become fluent with their knowledge, so that known information can be used to learn new things. Thus, the corner activities are about applying and transferring knowledge gained from assisted activities to independent work. As Julie glances around the room, she observes that the children are working on appropriate tasks that are aimed at their zones of actual development (see Chapter 1). Julie notes that some children are sorting letters into feature categories; some children are building high-frequency words with magnetic letters and recording them in personal dictionaries; and other children are working on word analysis activities with compound words, prefixes, and contractions (see Chapter 5 on literacy corners and task cards).

After lunch, Julie calls the class together for the afternoon whole-group meeting. This is a thirty-minute literacy block that begins with a read-aloud followed by a mini-lesson that introduces the writers' workshop. As the children gather around Julie, she captures their attention with a brief introduction to the new story. As she reads, she stops from time to time to engage the children in book discussions. She listens as they relate the story events to their own life or to other books that they have read. Julie knows that talking about books develops children's comprehension skills, increases their vocabulary knowledge, and builds story schema. Each day she ensures that her children will hear two or three texts read aloud to them.

When the read-aloud has ended, the children remain seated with the group. They know the routine well, for the next event is a whole-class mini-lesson that leads into the writers' workshop. Each day, the children are introduced to a new skill that will help them in their writing. Over the year, Julie's mini-lessons have covered a wide range of topics, including editing and revising skills, lead sentences, prewriting strategies, and publishing techniques. She has included lessons that focused on mechanical issues, such as spelling, punctuation, and capitalization. Today, Julie has prepared a mini-lesson that focuses on descriptive words. She has selected a favorite book that includes rich descriptions and guides her children to listen to

how the author has used words to paint pictures in the readers' minds. Then she demonstrates this process through her own think-aloud. She puts a phrase on the board and thinks aloud about words that she can use to paint pictures in the minds of her own readers. Julie's mini-lessons are brief and focused, so as not to overload the students with too many new things to learn. Last, she encourages the children to apply this strategy to their own writing.

As the mini-lesson ends, the children know that it is time for writers' workshop. Here, Julie understands that children must develop a habit of writing daily. The goal is that her children will value writing as a means of recording information and communicating ideas with others. Julie's writing curriculum is designed so that her children will learn the processes of writing, including brainstorming, writing first drafts, revising the message, editing for grammar and spelling, producing final drafts, and publishing for a specific audience. During this thirty-minute block of sustained writing, Julie holds individual conferences with students.

In this three-and-a-half-hour literacy block, Julie has provided her first graders with a background for learning about reading and writing. She knows that all new learning is grounded in old learning; thus she presents her students with a range of problem-solving opportunities that require them to use their knowledge in flexible ways. Julie's goal is to create learning conditions that engage the minds of her students in noting relationships between their reading, writing, and word-solving activities. Her curriculum for literacy is based on her understandings about children's literacy development, with high expectations for student achievement.

In Chapter 3, we focus on the characteristics of a literacy processing system and the changes that occur over time as children become more competent literacy learners.

Applying the Common Beliefs About Literacy Development to a First-Grade Program

Belief	*Daily Instructional Activity*
Children become better readers and writers with practice.	Independent reading of many easy or familiar books Guided reading of texts at instructional level Discussing books Guided problem solving during shared reading experiences
Reading and writing are reciprocal processes.	Shared reading experiences that link reading and writing processes Explicit teacher language that connects the two processes Small-group reading and writing lessons that bridge the two processes
Children's past experiences form a knowledge base for new learning.	Teacher bases all instruction on observations, running records, writing samples, literacy corner notebooks, and other ongoing documentation of student progress. Teacher designs activities at literacy corners to promote fluency, flexibility, and automaticity, with all activities linked to previous reading and writing experiences. Teacher selects spelling words from children's reading and writing texts and looks for other opportunities to spotlight the words in different places. Teacher prompts children to apply current strategies to problem-solve on unknown information.
Beginning readers should have many opportunities to learn about print.	Independent, guided, and shared reading Interactive writing experiences with explicit teaching of print concepts Independent writing with follow-up teacher conferences Letter-sorting and word-building activities in literacy corners Sentence and word-matching activities in literacy corners
Hearing books read aloud is a vital part of learning how to read.	Read-aloud experiences with book discussions
Children should engage in active book discussions and share their reading and writing with others.	Discussing texts in guided reading, literature groups, and read-aloud

	Making predictions before and during shared reading experiences
	Sharing published work in author's chair
	Sharing texts with peers during peer conferences
Reading is a meaning-making, problem-solving process.	Teacher prompts for strategies during reading and writing activities
	Revising texts for meaning, and editing writing for errors
	Solving problems in literacy corners
	Learning how to monitor, search, and self-correct when reading during guided reading
	Enhancing comprehension through story retellings
Beginning readers should have a well-designed phonics program.	Identifying and sorting letters at literacy corners
	Matching letters and sounds during spelling lessons
	Building high-frequency words during spelling and word-building activities
	Learning about word patterns during poetry and spelling lessons
	Locating letters and words during shared reading and guided reading lessons
	Learning about words in daily writing lessons
	Using word-solving strategies during guided reading lessons
Children should write every day.	Writing groups at children's instructional level
	Daily mini-lessons prior to writers' workshop
	Daily writers' workshop
	Daily conferences with individual students
	Daily independent writing in notebooks at literacy corners
	Writing to describe problem solving in spelling lessons

Shaping a Literacy Processing System

In this chapter, we continue to discuss the relationship between the literacy curriculum and children's literacy development. What are some observable behaviors that indicate how children are processing information at emergent, early, transitional, and fluent levels? This question implies that a change in literacy behavior is occurring as children become more proficient in specific reading and writing areas. It is important for teachers to recognize the signals that indicate children are gaining greater competence in these tasks. Is there a link between the types of instructional opportunities that children are provided and the development of their literacy knowledge? These questions provide a framework for exploring how children become literate and the role of the curriculum in shaping literate behavior.

A Literacy Continuum

We encourage teachers to study children's reading and writing progression along a literacy continuum. This concept allows us to examine the development of a literacy behav-

ior that changes over time as children acquire greater competence in given areas. Also, it means that teachers must look beyond grade-level expectations and focus more closely on the learning patterns of children. From this point of view, we can expect to see changes that occur along a continuum of learning control that is constantly in motion. For example, as children acquire a new skill, we observe a pattern of control that moves from approximated to refined to automatic (almost unconscious). In regard to teaching and learning, we can make four assumptions:

- The child will become more skillful and fluent in using her knowledge, skills, and strategies through successful and prolonged practice.
- The teacher will adjust her support to accommodate the child's increasing control.
- The teacher will raise the ante in such a way that the child is kept at the cutting edge of her learning development.
- The child will apply what she already knows to make sense of the new informa-

tion, thus gaining greater control over her own thinking processes.

Observable Changes Over Time

Recall that Figure 1.3 presented a developmental continuum of learning control, one that begins with awareness and ends with self-regulation. This is an important concept because all new learning is grounded in awareness. From awareness, children learn how to direct their attention to important and relevant aspects, and through successful practice, they gain greater control of the action. Let's look at a few examples that reflect change over time in literacy control:

- *Change over time in one-to-one matching control.* Movement from crisp finger pointing to flexible finger pointing to voice pointing to greater fluency with no overt pointing behaviors.
- *Change over time in fluent reading.* Movement from fluent enactment of the text with little attention to the printed word, to more word-by-word reading with close attention to the print, to fluent and expressive reading with self-regulated drops in fluency as needed to problem-solve on unknown words.
- *Change over time in phonological control.* Movement from hearing larger units within words (e.g., phrases, words, rhyming patterns, and syllables) to hearing the finer distinctions of the individual phonemes within the word.
- *Change over time in writing letters.* Movement from slow, laborious production of letter forms to fast and fluent production.
- *Change over time in recording words.* Movement from detailed attention to the word, including spelling or saying the word slowly, to fast recording of the word with minimal attention to the word itself.
- *Change over time in error detection.* Movement from no detection of error, to more overt signs of self-monitoring (e.g., hesitating, appealing), to self-correcting the error immediately afterward (postprocessing), to making fewer errors, which indicates the mind is preprocessing the information prior to making the error.
- *Change over time in rereading for confirming meaning.* Movement from rereading longer stretches of text, to rereading just a few words, to repeating the word as if to confirm the meaning.
- *Change over time in depth of reading comprehension.* Movement from literal-level recall with sequenced details to higher-level generalizations that go beyond the printed message.

Developing Orthographic and Phonological Systems

An important period in a child's literacy development is that short stretch of time when they crack the code. This is when they can develop independence and enthusiasm—or they can learn to see reading and writing as rote tasks. The role of the teacher is critical in guiding students to acquire effective strategies for solving the print-sound code. To illustrate specific changes that occur in the development of a literacy processing system at the print-sound level, we have outlined the connections between reading, writing, and orthographic knowledge at four points in literacy control: the emergent, early, transitional, and fluent levels. The acquisition of orthographic knowledge is influenced by the very acts of reading and writing; thus, as reading development occurs, a similar relationship is observed in writing and spelling development. Throughout this

Table 3.1 Approximate Levels Along a Literacy Continuum

Literacy System	Grade Levels	Benchmark Levels
Emergent	End of Kindergarten	Text levels A–B
Early	Beginning of grade 1	Text levels B–D
	Midyear of grade 1	Text levels E–G
Transitional	End of grade 1	Text levels H–I
Transitional	Beginning of grade 2	Text levels J–K
Transitional	End of grade 2	Text level M
Fluent	Beginning of grade 3	Text level N
Fluent	End of grade 3	Text level P

Adapted from Fountas and Pinnell (1999, 26).

chapter, we use two terms that describe how readers and writers apply strategies to words: *decoding strategies,* the process used by readers to analyze unknown words according to letter or letter parts, with the intention of determining the word's meaning; and *encoding strategies,* the process used by writers to transcribe an oral message into printed symbols, including sound-to-letter analysis for constructing unknown words and writing fluency for recording known words.

Two Things to Consider

In teaching for the development of a literacy processing system, two things must be considered: book selection and formal/informal assessments of literacy behavior.

Teachers must be able to select appropriate texts that promote a balance between fluent reading and problem-solving opportunities. There are resource guides, such as *Matching Books to Readers* (Fountas and Pinnell 1999) and *Reading and Writing Grade by Grade* (New Standards Primary Committee 1999), that can provide teachers with guidance for selecting leveled books for children. Table 3.1 relates the four phases of the reading continuum to grade

levels, with approximate benchmark levels at each grade.

In addition, teachers must be able to assess literacy behavior as it relates to developmental changes over time and across literacy tasks. They can use both formal and informal measures to study progressions in students' reading and writing development.

Formal and Informal Literacy Assessments

Formal reading and writing assessments occur at critical intervals in a child's literacy program. Generally, these assessments are used to determine appropriate placement for guided reading and assisted writing groups. They can be used during parent conferences and literacy team meetings to illustrate students' progress over time on standard reading and writing tasks. (Figure 3.1 shows an example of a literacy assessment log.)

Formal Reading Assessments
- Running records provide teachers with standardized tools for assessing students' independent use of strategies on texts of graded difficulty (see Clay 1993). They reflect reading accuracy, self-correction rates, and language fluency. Reading checklists provide teachers with a standard way of analyzing

Figure 3.1 Literacy assessment log.

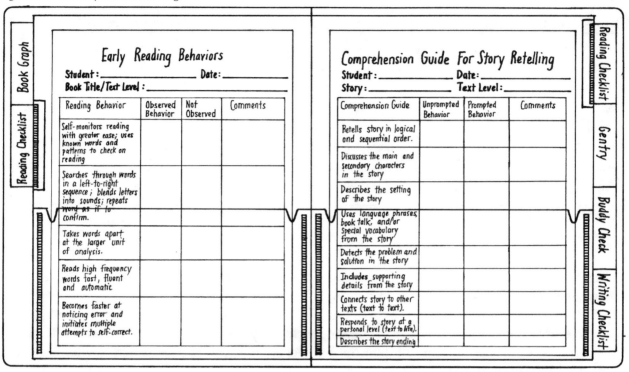

the visual strategies used by emergent and early readers as they problem-solve on continuous text.

- Retelling guides and comprehension prompts provide teachers with reliable measures for assessing students' comprehension.

Formal Writing Assessments

- Writing checklists provide teachers with a standard tool for analyzing students' writing samples based on a processing continuum, including analysis of print-sound control and the writing process.

- Writing rubrics provide teachers with standardized measures for assessing students' independent use of strategies on a range of writing tasks. They list specific behaviors that reflect proficiency along a writing continuum, including an understanding of the writing process, writing purposes, and language conventions.

Informal reading and writing assessments occur throughout the daily literacy block, including guided reading, reading conferences, literature discussion groups, assisted writing, and writers' workshop. Generally, these assessments are used to inform the teacher's daily decisions regarding students' reading and writing processes. These notes are written in the teacher's reading observation log and writing conference form.

Informal Reading Assessments

Reading observation logs provide teachers with ongoing documentation of students' processing on a variety of daily reading tasks, including running records, comprehension questions, literature discussion groups, and reading conferences.

Informal Writing Assessments

Students' writing portfolios and writing notebooks provide teachers with ongoing documentation of writing development.

A Literacy Processing System

From a cognitive perspective, a literacy processing system can be defined as a well-orchestrated internal network of interrelated information that works to construct meaning for a given event. Simply put, it is a fast reaction of the brain to resolve an immediate problem—a set of strategies that are initiated by the child to gain meaning for a text (Clay 1991). It is related to self-regulation (see Chapter 1), that is, an ability to monitor and guide learning processes across shifting circumstances. A literacy processing system develops through meaningful and relevant experiences over time. When children apply problem-solving strategies across reading and writing situations, the brain builds neural connections or pathways between these related sources of knowledge. In this way, if learners are unable to access the needed information through one channel, they can take an alternative route to solve the problem. Children building a literacy processing system may be considered to be at one of four levels: the emergent, early, transitional, or fluent level. The Appendix has reproducible copies of these tables to use in team meetings and to plan activities.

The Emergent Level

The print-sound knowledge of a child at the emergent level is shown in Table 3.2.

Table 3.2 Print-Sound Knowledge at the Emergent Level

Reading System	Orthographic System	Writing System
Attends to print using some known letters.	Analyzes letter features; identifies letters based on discriminating features.	Writes known letters with correct formation.
Points to words in a one-to-one match throughout one to three lines of patterned text.	Knows concept of word; constructs single-syllable words in left-to-right order.	Uses spaces between words with greater accuracy.
Recognizes link between known letters and related sounds; articulates first letter in unknown word.	Builds familiar words using slow articulation and direct letter-sound match in single-syllable words.	Recognizes link between known sounds and related letters; slowly articulates word with blended sounds.
Uses a special key word from ABC chart or letter book to help with solving unknown words.	Notices relationship between known letters and sounds as they relate to special key words.	Uses ABC chart and letter books as resources for sound-letter links.
Fluently reads some high-frequency words in easy texts; begins to acquire a reading vocabulary of about twenty frequently encountered words.	Constructs high-frequency words in left-to-right order; says word slowly and coordinates letter-sound match.	Writes a few high-frequency words with accuracy; begins to acquire a writing vocabulary that reflects attention to print during reading.
Self-monitors using high-frequency words and other known visual cues; rereads to cross-check first letter against meaning and structure cues.	Compares and categorizes words by initial sounds and basic rhyming patterns.	Uses first part of known words to help write parts of an unknown word.
Notices unknown words and guesses at the meaning from pictures or how the words are used in text.	Sorts words according to meaning classifications; expands word knowledge by noting meaningful relationships.	Includes new words from reading experiences in writing of texts.

Reading Strategies The goal of instruction at the emergent level is to create a textual context where children can learn how to attend to print. This means that the visual processing system must first be activated. The child must attend to the graphic symbols on the page, then relate the printed forms to a sequence of sounds that represent a meaningful word. The teacher can promote attending and searching behaviors by prompting the child to look for known letters or words within easy or familiar texts. For instance, after the child has just finished reading a book, the teacher might use a masking card to frame a known word and ask, "What is that word?" Other prompts might include "Can you find a word on this page that you know?" or "Can you find a word on this page that starts like your name?" Here, the child is learning how to search among a range of print cues for a familiar source, thus sharpening her attention to the print-sound code.

Yet, reading involves much more than just visual information; it includes a collection of knowledge, skills, and strategies with the goal of enabling a reader to construct meaning for a particular text. The challenge for the emergent reader is to learn how to integrate the meaning and structural cues from the text while simultaneously developing knowledge of the print-sound code.

At the emergent reading level, the teacher carefully selects easy texts with repetitive patterns that contain some letters and words that the child is beginning to notice. These print cues serve as visual anchors that allow the child to gain control of early behaviors, such as word-by-word matching, self-monitoring with known words, and using some known letters to solve unknown words. At the end of their kindergarten program, children should be able to read level B books that have been previously introduced to them in a guided reading setting.

Let's look at one example of an emergent reader.

✓ ✓ ✓
Come and see
✓   ✓
the monkey.
✓ ✓ ✓
Come and see
✓   ✓
the elephant.
✓ ✓ ✓
Come and see
✓   ✓
the kangaroos.
✓ ✓ ✓
Come and see
✓ <u>lion</u>
the tiger.
✓ ✓ ✓
Come and see
✓ ✓
the bear.
✓ ✓ ✓
Come and see
✓   ✓
the giraffe.
✓ ✓ ✓
Come and see
✓ _____ | A
the zebra. |
✓ ✓ ✓
Come and see
✓ <u>hippo</u> | SC
the hippopotamus.

Here, Clarissa is able to read a simple pattern book, *At the Zoo* (Randell, Giles, and Smith 1996), with 95 percent accuracy. She shows control of word-to-word matching and directional movement for two lines of text. She attends to some partially known words (*come, and, see, the*) that she uses to guide her reading activity.

When she approaches unknown words, Clarissa searches the picture cues and checks this information against her background knowledge. She readily accepts the substitution *lion* for *tiger* with little attention to the first-letter difference. She monitors the unknown word *zebra* by hesitating, searching the picture, and appealing for help when she is unable to recall the animal's name. And she quickly reads the word *hippo* for *hippopotamus*, then self-corrects the word with ease and confidence.

Clarissa's reading behavior provides Teresa, her teacher, with a context for studying how she is processing cues in continuous text. Teresa analyzes the child's reading behavior on the reading checklist (Figure 3.2) that she attaches to her running record. At other times during the day (during independent reading, guided reading, literacy corners), Teresa records the child's reading behaviors in her reading observation log (Figure 3.3). These formal and informal assessments provide Teresa

Figure 3.2 Reading checklist for an emergent reader. (Appendix A provides a blank form.)

Emergent Reading Behaviors: Attending to Print

Student Clarissa   **Date** Feb. 6, 1999

Book Title/Text Level At the Zoo/TL B

Reading Behavior	Observed Behavior	Not Observed	Comments
Attends to print using known words.	✔		Uses partially known words to monitor attention to print.
Points to words with 1-1 matching on 1 and 2 lines of text.	✔ ✔		Good pointing behavior on one-syllable words; holds finger in place on multi-syllabic words that fall at end of line. Return sweep okay.
Fluently reads some high-frequency words.	✔		Come, and, see, the
Articulates first letter in unknown words.		✔	
Notices unknown words and searches for cues in picture and print.	✔ ✔		zebra | T A hippo | SC hippopotamus |
Uses a special key word from ABC chart or letter book to help with solving words.		✔	
Rereads to cross-check first letter with meaning and structure cues.		✔	

Figure 3.3 Reading observation log.

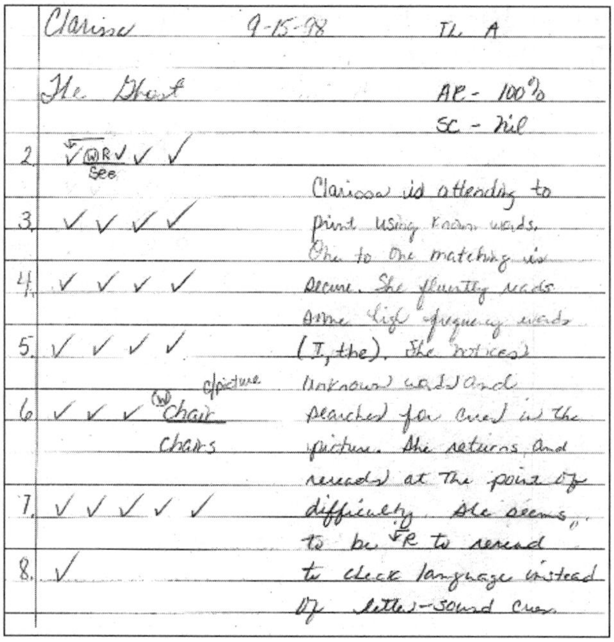

Figure 3.4 Writing sample from an emergent writer.

with a rich description for analyzing Clarissa's literacy development in different contexts and over time.

Writing Strategies During writing, the emergent reader is provided with similar opportunities to learn about print. For example, sounds are represented by letters; words are made of letters that occur in a left-to-right order; some words occur more often than other words; and whole words are separated by spaces. The child acquires strategies for solving words, such as saying words slowly to analyze the sequence of the sounds and using special print cues from reading as resources for sound-to-letter links. The orthographic system is strengthened through opportunities to analyze and sort letters according to particular features and build single-syllable words in a left-to-right sequence.

In this example of an emergent writer (Figure 3.4), we can observe how the child pro-

cesses the print—in a way that is similar to the reading process. Here, Matt has written an innovative text about the planet Neptune. His kindergarten class has been studying the planets, and the room is full of interactive writing texts, word charts, and Big Books that contain "space" words. In this writing sample, Matt utilizes available resources from previous reading (e.g., he copies the words *Neptune, found,* and *moon* from charts around the room). Through this action, he is developing an understanding of the links between the reading and writing processes. Furthermore, we can see that Matt is able to write several high-frequency words with accuracy (*went, the, to, on, I*). His teacher, Jan Allred, examines Matt's writing for evidence of his word-solving strategies. For instance, in his attempt to write the words *space by a rocket ship* (*spsbaritp*), he displays his ability to hear and record consonant sounds in sequence. This assumption is further supported by his sound-to-letter analysis on the words *landed* (*lD*) and *rocks* (*ros*). Jan records on the writing checklist (Figure 3.5) specific writing behaviors that she has observed from Matt's independent writing.

Figure 3.5 Writing checklist for an emergent reader. (Appendix B provides a blank form.)

Emergent Writing Behaviors: Encoding and Writing Fluency

Student ___Matt___   **Date** ___Feb. 6, 1999___

Written Text ___Planet (from science project)___

Writing Behavior	Observed Behavior	Not Observed	Comments
Writes known letters with correct formation.	✔		Fluent control of letters.
Uses spaces between words with greater accuracy.	✔		Understands concept of space. When he stopped to work on sounds, concept of space was ignored.
Recognizes link between known sounds and related letters; slowly articulates word with blended sounds.	✔ ✔		Able to hear and record most sounds in unknown words (<u>land</u>ed/<u>ld</u>; space/sps; by/b; rocket/rit; ship/p). Says words slowly to help with sound analysis.
Uses ABC chart or letter book as resource for sound-letter links.	✔ ✔		Uses ABC chart as reference; also copied words from wall (<u>Neptune</u>, <u>found</u>, <u>moon</u>).
Writes a few high-frequency words with accuracy; begins to acquire a writing vocabulary that reflects attention to reading.	✔ ✔		Writes known words with ease (<u>I</u>, <u>went</u>, <u>to</u>, <u>on</u>, <u>the</u>). Records words from reading (<u>Neptune</u>, <u>moon</u>, <u>found</u>) into writing.
Uses first part of known words to help write parts of unknown words.		✔	
Includes new words from reading experiences in writing.	✔		Records words from science chart into writing (<u>Neptune</u>, <u>moon</u>, <u>found</u>).

At the emergent level, the writer must deal with dual but complementary processes: the ability to compose a message while simultaneously learning how to transcribe the printed word. As teachers, we must be cautious that we do not negate one aspect of the writing process at the expense of the other. With Matt, his teacher recognized the two processes as critical components in the development of a writing system.

The Early Level

The print-sound knowledge of a child at the early level is shown in Table 3.3.

At the early level, the child can monitor his reading with greater ease, and, as a result, he can engage in more efficient searching behaviors to solve problems within text. As the reader practices these processing actions on texts that he can read at 94 percent accuracy or above, his searching and correcting behaviors

Table 3.3 Print-Sound Knowledge at the Early Level

Reading System	Orthographic System	Writing System
Self-monitors reading with greater ease; uses known words and patterns to check on reading; notices words within words; begins to acquire a reading vocabulary of about 150 words from easy and familiar texts.	Spells most unknown words phonetically, including embedded sounds in two- or three-syllable words; later, moves into transitional spelling, noticing common patterns from reading and writing; letter knowledge fast and automatic.	Begins to notice common misspellings in writing and searches through a simple dictionary for corrections; uses resources and checklists; acquires a writing vocabulary that reflects reading experience.
Searches through words in a left-to-right sequence; blends letters into sounds; repeats word as if to confirm identity.	Knows that letters come together in a left-to-right sequence; says words slowly to match letters to sounds; acquires knowledge of interletter relationships from building familiar words (*sh/she; th/the*).	Analyzes sequence of sounds and records corresponding letters; segments and blends sounds in words with increasing ease.
Takes words apart at the larger unit of analysis (consonant digraphs, inflectional endings, onset and rime patterns, blends).	Notices relationship between letter patterns and clusters of sounds; uses known words as a base for adding inflections.	Constructs words using larger units of sound-to-letter patterns; faster and more efficient at writing words.
Reads high-frequency words fast, fluently, and automatically.	Uses known patterns (onset and rime) to build unknown words.	Applies knowledge of onset and rime patterns for writing unknown words.
Becomes faster at noticing errors and initiates multiple attempts to self-correct.	Manipulates letters to form simple analogies.	Notices similarities between word patterns (*mother, father, over*).

become more refined. This knowledge frees up the reader's attention so that he can focus more on the comprehension process.

During this period, text reading levels span a large continuum of reading difficulty, beginning with text level B and ending with text level G (Fountas and Pinnell 1999; New Standards Primary Committee 1999). At the lower end of the continuum, the texts are similar to emergent-level books, with repetitive patterns and high picture support. Along this continuum of easy to harder texts, the modifications that occur in text organization should match the changes that occur in the students' reading control. For instance, we might expect to see some of the following adjustments in the text:

- Sentences become longer, with embedded clauses and connecting words.

- Structural patterns become more complex, including literary language and more abstract concepts.
- Picture cues change from detailed objects to supportive story ideas.
- Story lines shift from simple patterns to complex events and episodes.

To illustrate these changes along the literacy continuum, let's look at two examples that reveal the relationship between the text selection, the child's processing at each level, and the teacher's degree of support.

Beginning of the Early Level

In the first example, Kim is reading *Looking Down* (Smith 1996), a level C text. Although the book contains a repetitive pattern on most pages, the ending is designed to build suspense and engage the child in predicting the story's final episode. On the last two pages of the book, the illustrator has sprinkled clues into the pictures that signal a change in the story's pattern (e.g., the cat is chasing leaves; the girl turns her back to the street; the cat is gone; the cat is climbing the tree behind the girl; the cat is in the tree with the girl). Along with the picture support, the author has introduced a new type of textual cue, ellipsis dots (. . .), to signal the reader that an unexpected event is about to occur. In this simple pattern, the child is learning how to

- Use print-sound cues (e.g., monitor with known words and problem-solve on unknown words using known information)
- Apply comprehension strategies (e.g., predict events, make inferences; note cause-and-effect relationships)

The teacher assesses the child's processing at two levels: depth of comprehension after the text has been read (retelling and comprehension prompts), and decoding strategies used to problem-solve during the reading of the text. Let's look at Kim's performance on these two reading assessments, starting with the story retelling.

Comprehending the Text Comprehension is the ultimate goal of the reading act. A reliable measure for assessing a student's comprehension of a story is through a structured retelling. Here, the teacher first invites the student to retell the story with a simple prompt of "Tell me what happened in the story." If the student needs further help, the teacher increases her level of support by asking specific questions for assessing the student's comprehension. At the end of Kim's reading, the teacher uses the story retelling guide (Figure 3.6) to assess the

child's level of comprehension. For instance, her unprompted retelling indicates that Kim is able to independently recount the story events in sequential and logical order; her prompted retelling documents that Kim can identify—with teacher support—story elements such as character, problem, and solution.

Processing Behaviors on Text This running record illustrates how Kim processes the text information as she independently reads the new book,

✓ ✓ ✓ ✓   ✓
I can see my mom.
✓ ✓ <u>washing</u> ✓ ✓
She is cleaning the car.
✓ ✓ ✓ ✓ ✓
I can see my dad.
✓ ✓<u>d-digging</u> ✓   ✓
He is digging the garden.
✓ ✓ ✓ ✓   ✓
I can see my sister.
✓ ✓   ✓   ✓ ✓
She is reading a book.
✓ ✓ ✓ ✓   ✓
I can see my brother.
✓ ✓   ✓ ✓ ✓
He is riding a bike.
✓ ✓ ✓ ✓   ✓
I can see my grandfather.
✓ ✓ <u>raking</u>   ✓   ✓
He is sweeping the sidewalk.
✓ ✓ ✓ ✓ ✓
I can see my cat.
✓ ✓ ✓   ✓   ✓
She is chasing the leaves.
✓ ✓ ✓
I can see . . .
   ✓ ✓
. . . my cat!
✓ ✓ ✓   ✓ ✓
She is here with me.

Figure 3.6 Comprehension guide for story retelling. (Appendix C provides a blank form.)

Comprehension Guide for Story Retelling

Student ___Kim_____ Date ___Nov. 12, 1999_____

Story ___Looking Down_____ Text Level ___TL C_____

Comprehension Guide	Unprompted Behavior	Prompted Behavior	Comments
Retells story in logical and sequential order.	✔		
Discusses the main and secondary characters in the story.	✔		
Describes the setting of the story.		✔	"in the tree"
Uses language phrases, book talk, and/or special vocabulary from the story.	✔ ✔		"can see" "sweeping the sidewalk"
Detects the problem and solution in the story.			Problem not as obvious in this story.
Includes supporting details from the story.			Story didn't have a lot of details.
Connects story to other texts (text-to-text).			No
Responds to story at a personal level (text-to-life).		✔	"My cat likes to climb trees."
Describes the story ending.	✔		

and Figure 3.7 shows the reading checklist for the child's reading behavior. Her errors indicate that she understands meaning but is not attending to first-letter cues, for instance, *washing/cleaning, raking/sweeping.* Yet, when Kim approaches the word *digging* in the text, she hesitates and articulates the *d* sound, then rereads the sentence, and says the word correctly. This behavior reveals to her teacher that Kim can use the first letter as a checking source. Thus, the teacher validates the child's knowledge and prompts her to apply this same strategy to an error word.

Teacher: Let's look at this page right here. Can you find the part where you did some really good checking?

Kim: (*Points to* digging.)

Teacher: What helped you on that word?

Kim: I saw the *d* and it made me think of the word.

Teacher: Yes, you used two ways to help

Figure 3.7 Reading checklist for an early reader. (Appendix D provides a blank form.)

Early Reading Behaviors: Decoding Strategies

Student Kim   **Date** Nov. 12, 1999

Book Title/Text Level Looking Down/TL C

Reading Behavior	Observed Behavior	Not Observed	Comments
Self-monitors reading with greater ease; uses known words and patterns to check on reading.	✔ ✔		Good monitoring with known words. Substitutions are meaning and structural sound; also contain known parts (<u>ing</u>).
Searches through words in a left-to-right sequence; blends letters into sounds; repeats word as if to confirm.	✔	✔	Articulates first letter (<u>d</u>–<u>digging</u>); blends parts together and repeats word as if to confirm.
Takes words apart at the larger unit of analysis.		✔	
Reads high-frequency words fast, fluently, and automatically.	✔		Good, no hesitation. Also, good phrasing and fluent reading.
Becomes faster at noticing errors and initiates multiple attempts to self-correct.		✔	High accuracy rate (97%); did not self-correct errors. No evidence of multiple attempts at this time.

yourself there. You thought of what would make sense in the story, and you used the first letter. That was good checking. (*Turns to page where Kim substituted the word* rak-ing *for* sweeping.) Now, try this part again.
Kim: (*Reads it correctly.*) He is sweeping the sidewalk.
Teacher: What helped you there?
Kim: I thought of what would make sense and start with an *s*.

Writing Strategies Along the early literacy continuum, we can expect to see the children apply similar strategies across reading and writing. For instance, Courtney is reading *Caps for Sale* (Slobodkina 1987), a level D text. Her kindergarten teacher, Cassie Richardson, notes that Courtney demonstrates the following strengths in her writing (Figures 3.8 and 3.9):

- Able to respond to literature from a story that was read aloud to her

Figure 3.8 Writing sample from an early writer.

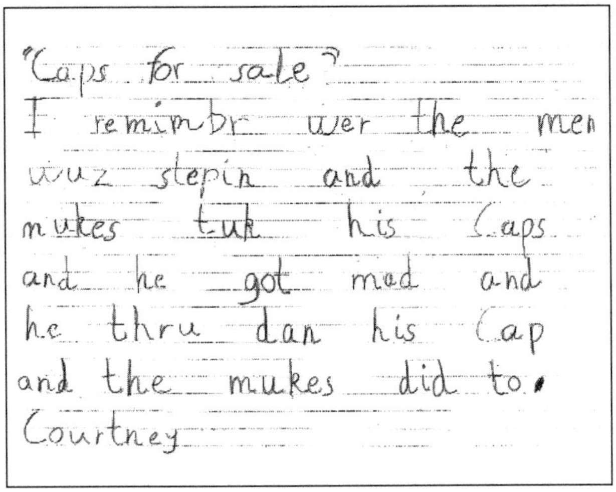
"Caps for sale"
I remimbr wer the men
wuz stepin and the
mukes tuk his Caps
and he got mad and
he thru dan his Cap
and the mukes did to.
Courtney

- Able to hear and record embedded sounds in two- and three-syllable words (*remember, sleeping, monkeys*)
- Able to write some high-frequency words with ease (*the, and, his, he, got*)
- Able to construct a series of thoughts in order and link them with connecting words (*and*)

Near the End of the Early Level

As children become more competent readers and writers, they begin to exhibit greater control of their own processing actions. Near the end of the early continuum, their decoding strategies become more sophisticated. Through reading many books, they acquire a repertoire of common words, and they begin to notice interletter relationships (e.g., *th, sh, ine*) within known words. As a result, their searching behaviors reflect their attention to larger units of visual patterns within unknown words.

Let's look at a reading and writing sample for a child near the end of the early literacy continuum. Here, we use examples from Carla's literacy assessment log to study how Aaron applies similar strategies across the three language events—reading, writing, and spelling. Since comprehension is the ultimate goal of the reading act, Carla assesses Aaron's understanding of the story both during and after the reading event.

Comprehending the Text Aaron is reading a mystery book entitled *The Missing Necklace* (Reading Unlimited 1976), a level H text. This is a story about a pig that attends a picnic lunch and loses her marshmallow necklace. At the comprehension level, the story requires the reader to make several inferences from the clues that are embedded in the text (e.g., marshmallows are edible; the animals are attending a picnic; the necklace is missing immediately after the lunch). Furthermore, this simple mystery is organized in such a way that the reader learns how to eliminate the suspects and solve the mystery as the story approaches the final act. This means that if the reader is focusing on the meaning-making process, we can expect him to discover the clues that lead to solving the problem. Aaron's comments reflect comprehension and evaluation as he reads and collects more information from the story. For instance, near the end of the story, he exclaims, "The pig ate her own necklace!" After the reading, Carla and Aaron engage in a brief conversation about the story. She comments, "You solved the mystery before the end of the story! That was good thinking. What clues did you notice that helped you?" Through this prompt, Aaron is learning more about the characteristics of mystery stories: his response includes references to the characters, a series of events, the problem, and the solution. Here, it is important to emphasize that teachers do not have to ask a series of comprehension prompts; rather, they should listen carefully to how children respond to the story and record this information in their comprehension guide.

Figure 3.9 Writing checklist for an early writer. (Appendix E provides a blank form.)

Early Writing Behaviors: Encoding and Writing Fluency

Student _Courtney_   **Date** _Jan. 10, 1999_

Written Text _Responding to Literature (Caps for Sale) Teacher Read-Aloud_

Writing Behavior	Observed Behavior	Not Observed	Comments
Begins to notice common mis-spellings, circles words that do not look right; uses a simple dictionary to self-correct; uses resources to self-check work; acquires a writing vocabulary that reflects reading.	✔ ✔	✔	No use of circling; editing; resources to help her. Spells many high-frequency words correctly.
Analyzes sequence of sounds and records corresponding letters; segments and blends sounds in words with greater ease.	✔		Records sounds in order; phonetic level in spelling; hearing embedded sounds in two- and three-syllable words; attending to vowels in middle positions.
Constructs words using larger units of sound-to-letter patterns; becomes faster and more efficient at writing words.	✔		Some beginning awareness of units (re-mim-br) (thr-u)
Applies knowledge of onset and rime patterns for writing unknown words.		✔	
Notices similarities between word patterns.		✔	

Processing Behaviors on Text In addition to comprehension, teachers must also examine children's problem-solving strategies with unknown words. Carla has recorded Aaron's progress in a reading checklist (Figure 3.10). He is able to read the text with 100 percent accuracy, fluently and with expression. However, he slows down to search more overtly into unknown words, using his finger to isolate specific parts and stressing these units with his voice, for instance, *sand-wich-es, ther-mos, chip-munk, de-tec-tive, rad-ish.*

Carla records specific behaviors that indicate how Aaron works out problems. She uses her understanding of the processing system at the early level to analyze his attempts. She looks for patterns in his responses that reveal how he solves unknown words. For instance, on a previous day, Aaron had independently read a level F book, *Cookie's Week* (Ward 1988), and Carla had recorded notes in her observation log (Figure 3.11). When she compares his reading behavior over several days, she observes a pattern of responding to unknown

Figure 3.10 Reading checklist for Aaron, an early reader.

Early Reading Behaviors: Decoding Strategies

Student Aaron   **Date** March 10, 1999

Book Title/Text Level The Missing Necklace/TL H

Reading Behavior	Observed Behavior	Not Observed	Comments
Self-monitors reading with greater ease; uses known words and patterns to check on reading.	✔ ✔		High accuracy rate (100%); expressive and fluent reading; self-monitoring with ease.
Searches through words in a left-to-right sequence; blends letters into sounds; repeats word as if to confirm.	✔ ✔ ✔		Searches through words at larger unit. Pulled out finger on de-tec-tive and ran it through the word in L-to-R order, saying the word in parts; repeats word each time to confirm meaning. Stresses word parts with voice, but blends the parts back together as a smooth word unit.
Takes words apart at the larger unit of analysis.	✔		All analysis of unknown words is at the larger unit (sand-wich-es; ther-mos; chip-munk; de-tec-tive; rad-ish).
Reads high-frequency words fast, fluently, and automatically.	✔		Good, no hesitation. Also, good phrasing and fluent reading.
Becomes faster at noticing errors and initiates multiple attempts to self-correct.	✔		High accuracy rate indicates preprocessing before error is made. No errors, but evidence of problem-solving on unknown words. Hesitates on radish (unsure of concept?), searches picture, then breaks word apart, repeats whole word.

words that indicates his ability to "take words apart using larger units."

Writing Strategies In writing, Aaron shows similar behaviors as in reading. His writing sample, taken five days later from writers' workshop, indicates a high degree of independent problem solving (Figure 3.12). His story is based on a guided reading book from a previous day. From this sample, we can infer Aaron's strengths in the following areas:

- Uses a lead sentence that shows his experience with texts (*Once upon a time*)
- Revises word attempts immediately after the error (*thai/there; cr/crall; reversed G/g; su/some; goi/gulped, untill/until*)
- Uses complex sentence structures (*as he grabbed the fish with his huge pinchers*)
- Applies a variety of punctuation (quotation marks, exclamation point, ellipsis dots, periods)
- Edits most misspelled words by circling them

Figure 3.11 Reading observation log for Aaron.

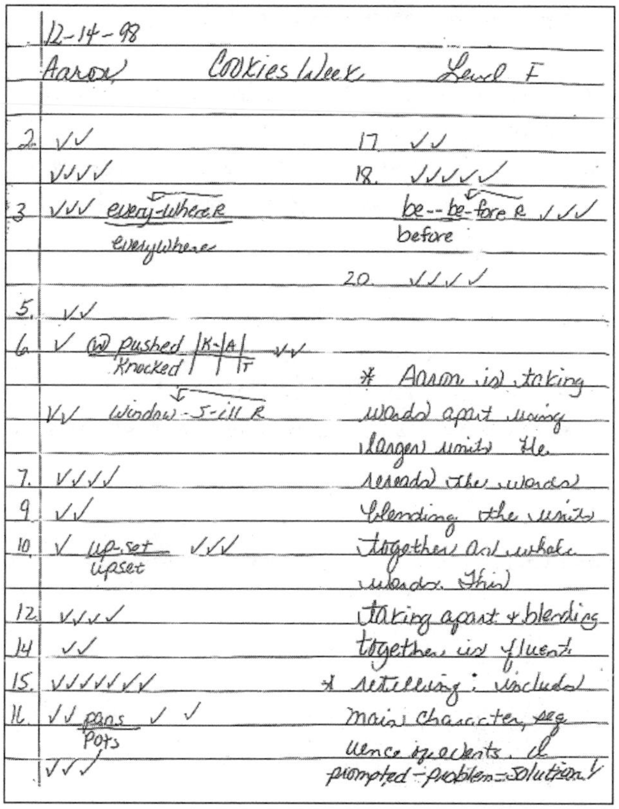

Figure 3.12 Aaron's independent writing.

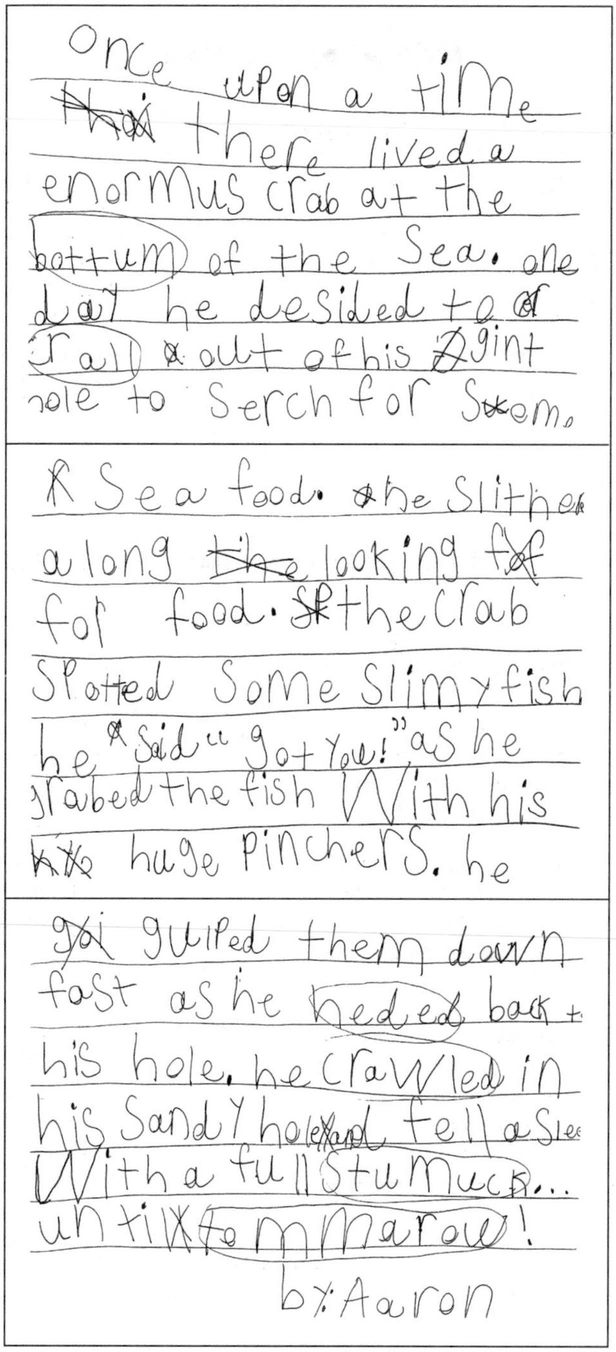

- Revises the message to enhance meaning immediately following the error (*fof/for food*)
- Applies a writing vocabulary that reflects his reading vocabulary (*slithered, enormous, decided, slimy, spotted, sandy*)

Figure 3.13 further illustrates Aaron's knowledge about words. Carla recorded her assessment of Aaron's story on a narrative writing checklist (Figure 3.14) and conducted an editing conference with Aaron. Prior to the conference, Aaron recorded his misspelled words on his trial page. In the Second Try column, he has attempted to correct these words and has highlighted the part of the word that has given him difficulty (see Chapter 4 on spelling workshop).

Figure 3.13 Aaron's spelling trial page.

My Spelling Trial Page — Aaron		
First Try	**Second Try**	**Correct**
boHum		
ctall	crawlʳ	crawl
heded	headed✓	headed
crawled	crawled	crawled
stumuck		
tommarow	tommorow	tomorrow

The following conference illustrates how Carla reinforces his word-solving strategies:

Teacher: Show me the part in the word that you had to think about.
Aaron: I wasn't sure if *crawl* had an *al* or *aw* in it. But when I tried it out, it looked better with *aw*.

Carla validates Aaron's checking behavior and coaches him to apply this strategy to the word *tomorrow*. She recalls that he is able to solve unknown words in his reading by taking them

Figure 3.14 Writing checklist for narrative writing. (Appendix F provides a blank form.)

Writing Checklist for Narrative Writing (Purposes and Craft)

Student: Aaron   Date: April 12, 1999

Text: The Enormous Crab (Story Innovation)

Writing Behavior	Observed Behavior	Not Observed	Comments
Uses an interesting introduction that grabs the attention of the reader.	✔		"Once upon a time, there lived an enormous crab at the bottom of the sea."
Writes events and ideas in logical and sequential order that makes sense to the reader.	✔		Story flows in a logical and sequential order, keeps the reader actively involved.
Sustains the idea throughout the piece.	✔		Nice work.
Uses dialogue.	✔		"Got you!"
Uses strong vocabulary and good word choices.	✔		Enormous, giant, decided, search, slithered, spotted, slimy, grabbed, huge, gulped, sandy.
Uses individual voice.	✔		"Got you!" Also, shows influence of book voice.
Uses reaction phrases.		✔	
Uses transition and time cue words to support flow.	✔		Sophisticated use of time elements: "Once upon a time"; "one day"; "as he grabbed"; "tomorrow."
Ties story together with creative or imaginative ending.	✔		"fell asleep with a full stomach . . . tomorrow."

apart at the larger unit of analysis. Therefore, she guides him to use this same strategy to analyze word parts (syllables) for spelling unknown words in his writing.

Teacher: Let's look at *tomorrow*. (*Points to the first and second attempts in his practice columns.*) Now, something about that word doesn't look right. Can you find it?

Aaron: I don't think it should have two *m*'s.

Teacher: Try it with only one *m*, and let's look at both spellings.

Aaron: (*Writes the word correctly in the final column.*) I think that one looks right.

Teacher: Draw a line between the three parts that you can hear in the word. Then see which parts look right to you.

Here, Carla wants Aaron to compare his knowledge of word parts. Which parts are log-ical units? Which parts are not? As soon as he draws the line between the syllables, he points to the two *m*'s in the middle syllable and exclaims, "No! That part looks funny!" "You're right," confirms Carla. "A syllable would not begin with two *m*'s. You're using something you know about word parts to help you with your spelling. That's good thinking!"

These examples from reading, writing, and spelling provide his teacher with further evidence of how Aaron applies similar problem-solving strategies across the three literacy events. These are the behaviors that we would expect a proficient first-grade student to use at the end of the early level.

The Transitional Level

The print-sound knowledge of a child at the transitional level is shown in Table 3.4.

Table 3.4 Print-Sound Knowledge at the Transitional Level

Reading System	Orthographic System	Writing System
Expands reading vocabulary; shows interest in unfamiliar words that are read to them.	Analyzes unknown words with greater efficiency and speed.	Expands writing vocabulary; includes new and unusual words.
Solves multisyllabic words by noticing parts within the words.	Uses syllable breaks to spell longer words.	Attends to syllables when writing words.
Quickly takes words apart on the run while reading.	Uses more complex analogies to analyze words.	Problem-solves with greater ease and fluency.
Reads longer texts with greater accuracy and fluency.	Analyzes parts of words (inflectional endings, rimes, contractions).	Writes increasingly longer texts with greater accuracy and speed.
Uses word meanings to solve word problems (prefixes, suffixes, roots, compound parts).	Classifies words according to meaningful parts.	Shows flexibility with word choice; tries out different ways of saying a message with the same meaning; revises word choices in writing process; uses a thesaurus as a resource.
Preprocesses error before making a mistake.	Spells words with greater accuracy; shows evidence of transitional spelling of words with more unusual patterns.	Uses dictionaries, editing checklists, and other resources to self-correct writing.

At the transitional level, the reader has developed a range of flexible strategies for working on text. He has acquired an extended reading vocabulary and shows interest in unfamiliar words that are read to him. His decoding skills are more sophisticated and refined; thus he reads longer texts with greater accuracy and fluency. He takes words apart on the run when reading and uses word meanings to solve unknown words. At the transitional level, the reading process is well-orchestrated, with greater attention paid to higher-level comprehension strategies. Here, we look at an example of a transitional reader—his comprehension strategies and his processing behaviors on text.

Comprehending the Text   Nathan is reading *Nate the Great and the Pillowcase* (Sharmat and Weinman 1993), a level K text. In this story, Rosamond calls Nate in the middle of the night to find her cat's missing pillowcase. Big Hex, the cat, likes to sleep on it, and he is pacing the floor, unable to sleep. Nate and his dog, Sludge, go out into the night to recover the missing pillowcase. The text is full of describing words— words that create images in the reader's mind, for example, *slashed, shredded, shrunken, shriveled* (to describe the pillowcase) and *damp, dreary, shivery* (to describe the night). Also, the author has placed clues throughout the story to help the reader solve the mystery. These challenges (at both the word and text levels) require the transitional reader to use a range of higher-level comprehension strategies:

- Construct inferences based on prior experiences and knowledge
- Make logical and reasonable assumptions based on a cumulative pattern of evidence
- Confirm or reject predictions as further evidence is presented
- Link clues to the unsolved mystery, thus learn about cause-and-effect relationships

- Form generalizations, such as text-to-text and text-to-life connections
- Summarize events

The teacher observes the child during the reading act and periodically checks his comprehension. For instance, if the child becomes too focused on word solving and neglects the story's meaning, the teacher might say, "Tell me what you just read on that page."

Processing the Text   Processing on words at the transitional level should not be a problem. Along the literacy continuum at the lower levels, the child has learned strategies for solving words with greater efficiency and ease. The reading observation log in Figure 3.15 notes that Nathan's accuracy rate was nearly perfect, with only two errors (a substitution of *the/this out/outside*). Nathan read the story with fluency and obvious enjoyment. He hesitated when he came to the words *dreary* and *shivery*, attempted to break the words into parts, looked puzzled, and reread the phrase. We can assume that his hesitation was influenced by the meaning of the words rather than by decoding difficulties. Even after his correct pronunciations, his voice indicated some uncertainty with his final choices. With higher-level texts, we can expect a richer vocabulary that can challenge children to examine the meanings of words. In this simple text, Nathan had to deal with meaningful associations for words, for example, "sleepy and strange, but not in that order." What do the words mean in the story? Similarly, the words that are used to describe the night are intended to create mental images to enhance the meaning of the story. Why would Nate go out on such a bad night? Although a good decoder can read the words with ease, their meanings can easily slip past the mind of the reader. Here, the teacher realizes that an important behavior for transitional

Figure 3.15 Reading observation log for Nathan, a transitional reader.

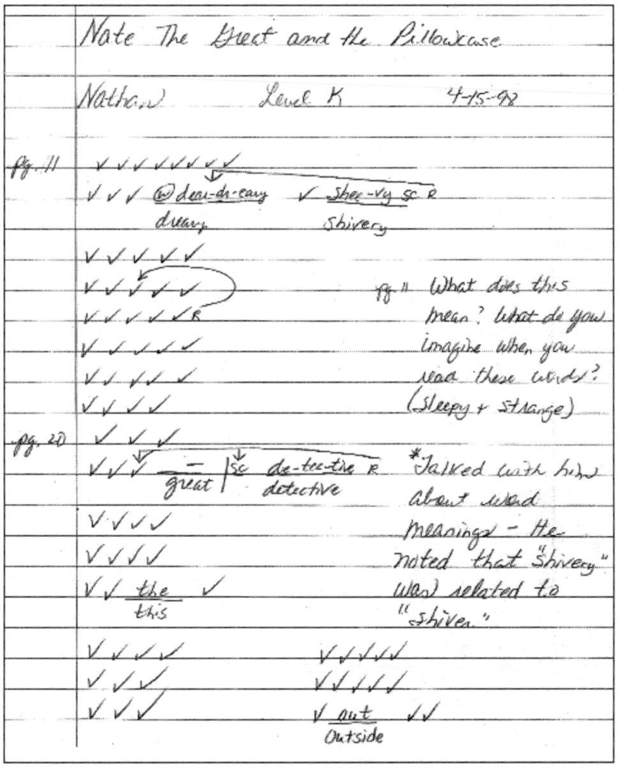
Nate The Great and the Pillowcase
Nathan Level K 4-15-98
pg. 11 ✓✓✓✓✓✓✓✓
✓✓✓ dear-dr-eary / dreary ✓ Shee-vy SC R / shivery
✓✓✓✓✓✓
✓✓✓✓✓✓ pg. 11 What does this mean? What do you imagine when you read these words? (sleepy + strange)
✓✓✓✓✓R
✓✓✓✓✓
✓✓✓✓✓
✓✓✓✓
pg. 20 ✓✓✓
✓✓✓ — / great SC de-tec-tive R / detective *Talked with him about word meanings – He noted that "shivery" was related to "shiver."
✓✓✓✓
✓✓✓✓
✓✓ the / this ✓
✓✓✓✓✓ ✓✓✓✓✓
✓✓✓ ✓✓✓✓✓
✓✓✓ ✓ out / Outside ✓✓

readers is to explore the meanings of words. Thus, with Nathan, the teacher concludes the running record with a comment about word meanings: "Can you read this part again and talk about what the words mean? How did the writer use these words to describe the night?" As Nathan rereads the text, he comments, "It was a wet night, but I'm not sure what *shivery* means." Then, he stops and exclaims, "Oh, it's cold! Because I shiver when I'm cold, so the night must be cold and shivery!" The teacher praises him: "Yes, you are using something you know about the meaning of another word to help you here." Comprehension is enhanced as children think about word meanings.

Writing Strategies At the transitional level, as with other levels, the writing process reflects the reading process. Here, the writer has acquired a repertoire of flexible strategies for making meaning and problem solving throughout the text. She has developed a habit of writing and understands the writing process. She carries a writing notebook around with her, recording her impressions and ideas as they occur. Her writing vocabulary reflects her reading experiences, including new and unusual words and figurative and literary language. She experiments with word choices and tries out different ways of communicating a message. She understands the writing process, including first drafts, revising, editing, and publishing. She is more aware of the craft of writing, and she incorporates techniques from her favorite authors into her own writing. She problem-solves with greater ease on words; her spelling reflects more accuracy and speed; and she writes increasingly longer texts.

Let's look at an example of a transitional writer from Patricia Robinson's first-grade writers' workshop (Figures 3.16 and 3.17). Here, Bethany reveals her understanding of the writing process: composing a first draft, revising for meaning, and editing for spelling. She adds a title, *In the Dark and Gloomy Woods;* she identifies her piece as a "fiction story"; and she concludes her writing with "The End." Her text is well-organized with lots of details, including rich describing words (e.g., *the meanest, biggest; growling and showing their big teeth*), strong action verbs (e.g., *bounded up the mountain; leaped across sharp stones; shrieked; screamed*), expressive language (e.g., *right then and there; going in circles; Sean's voice went low*), and transitional cues to signal time elements (e.g., *once, until, then*). Her writing incorporates a variety of sentence patterns and lengths; and she uses a range of punctuation, including commas, quotation marks, periods, and exclamation points. Her personal voice shows in her writing, as well as her experiences from reading lots of books.

Figure 3.16 Bethany's independent writing.

Writen and toled by By Bethany   a fiction story

In the dark and gloomy woods Once upon a ti time some warjors (traveled) into the woods. One warjor said, "It's dark in theese woods" "I The other warioŕ said, "Well I'm not scared, are you "no" then off they went (until) they got lost. antT A warior named Sean said, "I think were lost don't you." A nother warior named Jana who was a girl said, "Yes I do, I think we've (bin) going in (serecl) Then they herd a loud howling noes" or-ar-ar-oooo." "A wolf oh-no run hid (scrimed) Jana "It's okay "said Sean." I'll shout it whiwith my bow and arow and get it away. swoosh! the arow

flew into the air and hit the wolf in the back "arooo" said wolf as he feal to the grouned ground and (rite) then and there a hole pack of wolfs came leaping from (behined) a cliff. growling and showing its big teeth. And Then the meenest bigest jumped out and (atacked) Sean and mad a be big claw mark on him. "ow grows" siad said "he help me" Sean's (voes) went low "oh-no." (shicked) Jana," I must help him". She (leaped) across sharp stones She (bowned) up the (moratom) and then

She saw that Sean was okay and all they needed to do was: go home and (ban dag) up his (scar) when the two warrior's got back he home the (Andian's) had started a (powow) and started dancing around the fire singing: ah-a-ah-a-ah-a-aaaah. they welcomed home Sean and Jana and fixed Sean's (scar)

The End

Figure 3.17 Writing checklist for narrative writing for Bethany, a transitional writer.

Writing Checklist for Narrative Writing (Purposes and Craft)

Student ___Bethany_____   Date ___March 15, 2000_____

Text ___In the Dark and Gloomy Woods (fiction story)_____

Writing Behavior	Observed Behavior	Not Observed	Comments
Uses an interesting introduction that grabs the attention of the reader.	✔		Title sets the tone for the story (Dark and Gloomy Woods). Lead sentence places the travelers in this context; sets up reader expectation.
Writes events and ideas in logical and sequential order that makes sense to the reader.	✔		
Sustains the idea throughout the piece.	✔		
Uses dialogue.	✔		Uses dialogue to build suspense and enhance meaning.
Uses strong vocabulary and good word choices.	✔		Strong action words (traveled, shrieked, bounded, leaped). Good descriptors ("sharp stones," "Sean's voice went low") to create images.
Uses individual voice.	✔		"Oh, gross," "Sean was okay."
Uses reaction phrases.		✔	
Uses transition and time cue words to support flow.	✔		Sophisticated use of time elements: as, until, then and there.
Ties story together with creative or imaginative ending.			

The Fluent Level

The print-sound knowledge of a child at the fluent level is shown in Table 3.5.

Reading Strategies At the fluent level, the processing system is working with greater efficiency on harder texts. Here, the earlier behaviors—those acquired through daily reading habits and good processing actions—have prepared the reader for the challenges of more complex literacy tasks. The student reads longer texts with specialized content and unusual words. Her decoding skills are more automatic and she rarely makes errors in word solving. She has an extensive reading vocabulary; she applies knowledge of word meanings to unknown words; and she notices meaningful relationships between words, for example, similes, metaphors, and figurative language. She is comfortable with using a range of resources for reading and writing, such as dictionaries, thesauruses, encyclopedias, and other research materials. The fluent

Table 3.5 Print-Sound Knowledge at the Fluent Level

Reading System	Orthographic System	Writing System
Has an extensive reading vocabulary; reads longer texts with specialized content and unusual words; learns new words daily.	Has flexible control of spelling patterns; knows when words do not look right; can spell most words with minimal attention.	Has an extensive writing vocabulary; writes longer texts with good word choices; uses new words from reading.
Applies knowledge of word meaning to reading texts with more complex language structures.	Classifies words according to word meanings, including figurative and descriptive language.	Uses figurative language (similes, metaphors) and descriptive phrases to enhance message.
Responds to reading at many different levels; applies knowledge about word meanings across different texts; makes predictions about word meanings and checks within texts; refines word knowledge.	Notices multiple meanings of words; acquires a mental dictionary of word meanings.	Uses a range of resources, including thesaurus, dictionary, encyclopedia, and other research materials to plan and inform writing.

reader shows the characteristics of a lifelong learner, with a habit of reading and writing that is embedded in all aspects of her daily life.

Although the fluent system continues into the upper grades, we are focusing on the primary years. Thus, we mention one example of a typical text for a third-grade reader. Here, Jessica is reading a Nancy Drew mystery entitled *The Hidden Treasures* (Keene 1998), an S level text. In this book, Nancy has found an old diary full of secret clues, and she turns her school project into a treasure hunt. The author includes a series of clues for the reader to access in solving the mystery. At the fluent level, the reader has acquired a wealth of knowledge about text characteristics and authors' styles. She engages in book discussions with her peers, compares different genres, conducts literature extension activities, and records her impressions and ideas in her literature response log. She selects books based on summaries from the book jacket and her experiences with other books by the same author. She applies sophisticated comprehension strategies as she reads the text. She is an avid reader who reads at least thirty chapter books a year.

Angela Owen, the teacher, conducts a reading conference with Jessica and takes a running record on a few pages from the text. Jessica brings her book to the conference along with her conference guide. Angela prompts Jessica for comprehension, for instance, she asks questions such as, "What has happened in the story so far?" or "Where is your favorite part?" Angela records notes in her observation log. Then she asks Jessica, "Were there any words that you had difficulty with?" Here, Jessica turns to page 31 and points to the word *Almanac*. Angela prompts the student to read the page, and she takes a running record. Jessica reads the page with fluency and phrasing. When she comes to the word *Almanac,* she pronounces it as al-*man*-ac, with stress placed on the wrong syllable. Angela realizes the problem is not with decoding but rather with word meaning and pronunciation. Thus, in the follow-up discussion, she talks with the student about the meaning of the word.

Writing Strategies At the fluent level, the student demonstrates a good understanding of the writing process, including the crafts of writing. She uses a writer's log as a special notebook to record her observations and ideas. She writes for different purposes and a range of audiences. She develops a topic and uses strong vocabulary to express the precise message. She reflects and evaluates her writing according to high standards.

Sherwood, a fluent writer, uses personification to describe her experiences as a butterfly:

Butterflies

I was sitting in my egg all stuffed in a ball. It was real dark and cold and I was very scared. I was wondering when I would get out of here.

Finally the big day came, it was the day I popped out of my egg. I opened my eyes and saw beautiful things in the air. I looked at my body really close and I was black with a yellow and green stripe on my back, and lots of hair. I thought I was the best looking thing since Linda Evans.

After a couple of days of looking around the world, I opened my mouth to bite a leaf and a silver string came out of my mouth. I didn't know what was going on. I thought I might be sick with tongue cancer or something. Suddenly I had no control and this string started to wrap me up like a ball and it was like I was being inside my egg again.

When I got in this thing, I went to sleep for about six days and didn't even wake up to eat. When I woke up I thought it must be time to get up and I was ready because I was hot, sticky, stiff and everything ugly you can think of. It started to peel off and I could feel the breeze, see the trees and oh I saw some beautiful things with wings. I wished that I could look like that but I felt weak and weary and knew I could not ever be that beautiful.

After about five minutes I felt very strong with a great feeling in my body, so I jumped off the tree and discovered that I could fly.

I flew off with the other flying objects and say myself in a car window and saw that I was a butterfly, oh how pretty I was! That was the happiest day of my life.

In her piece, Sherwood employs figurative language, strong vocabulary, reactionary phrases, and personal voice. Her lead sentence introduces the setting and uses descriptive words that create a feeling of fear and uncertainty. Throughout her composition, she uses transitional words (e.g., *finally, after, when*) to create time flow in her writing. She includes details to develop her topic, she sticks with her theme, and she uses imagery to create pictures in the minds of her readers.

Closing Thoughts

Children become literate through active experiences with literacy. During guided reading and writing activities, children learn how to make connections between their reading and writing knowledge. Reading and writing are interrelated literacies that provide feedback and feedforward information for each other. This means that teachers must design reading experiences that are grounded in children's knowledge about writing, and vice versa. Yet, too often, in schools we find that reading, writing, and spelling are taught as separate activities, depriving children of opportunities to learn how to build literacy bridges between the processing systems.

In this chapter, we have discussed typical behaviors along a literacy continuum that reflects increasing control as children acquire new competence and strategies for problem solving in texts. Earlier, we discussed three levels of word knowledge, with orchestration representing the highest level of cognitive control. This means that students must develop self-regulated literacy systems that enable them to guide and monitor their knowledge across reading, writing, and spelling events. Also, it means that we, as teachers, must be able to recognize the changes that occur over time as children become more accomplished at literacy tasks. In the next chapter, we continue this discussion as we examine the relationship of spelling instruction to the development of a literacy processing system.

Developing Orthographic and Phonological Knowledge

In the previous chapter, we discussed the literacy processing system as it develops within the context of reading and writing. In this chapter, we continue the discussion but focus primarily on the phonological and orthographic sides of the language system. Teachers must recognize the developmental changes that occur over time as the print-sound system becomes more sophisticated. From a cognitive perspective, assessment informs instruction, and instruction causes developmental changes in learning. Therefore, in planning a spelling program, teachers must ask three important questions:

What can the child do independently?
(Actual level of development)
What can the child do with my help?
(Potential level of development)
What is too hard for the child to understand? (Frustration level of development)

Let's begin by discussing six important beliefs that relate to the development of a spelling system. We'll discuss each belief in depth, then apply these beliefs to the practical aspects of the daily spelling program.

Common Beliefs About Spelling

1. _Spelling instruction should be grounded in cognitive theories of perception, concentration, and organization of patterns_. The first step in spelling development is perception. Simply put, cognitive development depends on the input of perceptual (visual) stimuli from the printed word. Teachers must observe children as they respond to print symbols. Questions to ask are

What is the child attending to in the print?
What does he notice?
What does he _not_ notice?
What does he confuse?
Is there a pattern in his responses?

In learning about letters, perception involves attending to the distinctive features of the letter form. For instance, what feature defines the difference between an _e_ and _c, d_ and _b, r_ and _n_? Figure 4.1 shows some distinctive

55

Figure 4.1 Some distinctive features of letters.

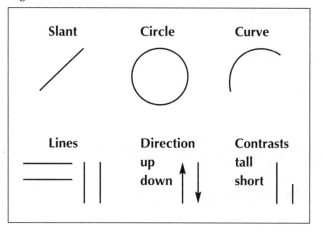

Figure 4.2 Cedric's writing sample.

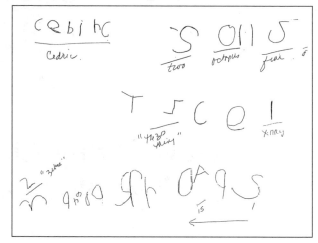

features of letters—circles, curves, angles, contrasts, and directional patterns. It is through the unique combination of these forms that a letter takes on its identity. When children learn how to analyze these features of letters, they notice the finer distinctions that occur between the letter shapes. Letter learning progresses from a primitive classification of similarities to an analytical comparison of differences.

For example, on the letter identification test, Cedric, a first-grade student, was able to identify only five letters. At first glance, his responses appeared random, but upon closer examination, each attempt could be categorized into a logical though primitive system of similarities. His responses to letters indicated three major categories: reversed orientation (*E/W*; *d/p*; *b/d*; *q/p*), removed fragment (*h/n*; *r/n*; *v/w*; *c/e*; *J/I*; *P/D*; *H/A*; *B/E*; *F/B*; *S/C*; *O/C*), and a mixture of both categories (*t/j*; *L/T*). Furthermore, his attempts indicated a logical though inaccurate set of associations from his classroom environment, for instance, geometric shape (*O/circle*), number (*1/l*), letter-sound (*K/C*), and alphabetic language chant (*L/LMNOP*). A further analysis of his writing provided additional evidence of what he was noticing about letters, attention to

curves dominating his perceptions of print (Figure 4.2). If we look closely at his name, we can see that the curve is an outstanding feature that occurs in *c, e, d, r, c*. Here, it is important to note that our brains group stimuli together by their similarities but retrieve them by their differences. Cedric, like many other children, was not attending to the visual differences in similar forms. Through letter sorting and classifying activities that focused his attention on the differences in print, Cedric quickly gained control of letter knowledge. Using the letters from his name (a familiar word), Linda asked differentiating prompts such as Can you find a curved letter? Can you find another curved letter? What part is the same? What part is different? Use your finger to trace over the part that is different. Trace over the part that is the same.

Research on beginning reading indicates that letter knowledge is a strong predictor of children's success in reading. However, letter learning is not a memorization task but a systematic process whereby children learn how to analyze the features of letters. When children write letters, they must attend to the detail of the features. Here, teachers use explicit language prompts that focus children's attention on the formation of letters, specifically, the movement pattern that occurs as a letter is being written (Table 4.1). As children become more automatic with letter knowledge, they begin to notice how letters come together in left-to-right sequence to represent whole words. In the process, they learn that words contain predictable and recurring spelling patterns. They attend to larger units within words (e.g., syllables, onset and rime, blends, inflectional endings), and they note relationships between clusters of letters and chunks of sound. This perceptual network enables children to use a more economical strategy for processing orthographic information with increased speed and accuracy.

2. *Children should learn problem-solving strategies for spelling words.* If children know some important words by heart and they understand how the spelling system works, they have the resources for spelling any new word they might encounter. For beginning

Table 4.1 Language Prompts for Movement Patterns to Form Letters

Teaching suggestions—As you describe the path of movement, stretch your voice to coordinate with the construction of the form.

     Example: (h) dow . . . n, up and over

                 (n) down, up and over

Although the path of movement is the same with both letters, "down" is stretched for the letter *h* to indicate a longer stroke.

A	slant down, slant down, across	a	over, around and down
B	down, up around, around	b	dow . . . n, up and around
C	over, around and open	c	over, around and open
D	down, up, around	d	over, around, u . . . p and down
E	down, across, across, across	e	across, over, around and open
F	down, across, across	f	over, dow . . . n, across
G	over, around, across	g	over, around, dow . . . n and curve
H	down, down, across	h	dow . . . n, up and over
I	down, across, across	i	down, dot
J	down, curve	j	down, curve, dot
K	down, slant in, slant out	k	dow . . . n, slant in, slant out
L	down, across	l	dow . . . n
M	down, slant down, slant up, down	m	down, up, over, up, over
N	down, slant down, up	n	down, up, over
O	over, around, close	o	over, around, close
P	down, up, around	p	dow . . . n, up, around
Q	over, around, close, slant out	q	over, around, down
R	down, up, around, slant out	r	down, up, curve
S	over, around, curve	s	over, around and curve
T	down, across	t	down, across
U	down, curve up	u	down, curve up, down
V	slant down, slant up	v	slant down, slant up
W	slant down, slant up, slant down, slant up	w	slant down, slant up, slant down, slant up
X	slant down, slant across	x	slant down, slant across
Y	slant down, slant up, down	y	slant down, slant dow . . . n
Z	across, slant down, across	z	across, slant down, across

spellers, here are four important principles that children need to understand:

- The letters are written to represent spoken sounds.
- The letters should be written in the same sequence in which the sounds are spoken.
- Some letters are combined to form patterns that represent certain pronunciations in a single syllable.
- Some words occur a lot and need to be remembered as a whole.

Based on these principles, children are taught strategies for learning how words work. At the emergent level, they learn to say a word slowly and listen to the sounds in it. The teacher asks a simple prompt that promotes sound-to-letter analysis: "Say the word slowly, and listen to what you can hear." At the semiphonetic level, children can hear beginning, middle, and ending consonant sounds, although not in sequence. As they become more competent at sound-to-letter analysis, children can hear and record most of the sounds within a word, including short-vowel sounds. Furthermore, they learn that sounds and letters must occur in a left-to-right order, and they expect to see a sequenced pattern of letters within familiar or partially known words. As a result, the teacher adjusts her coaching prompts to accommodate this higher level of perceptual analysis: "What can you hear next? Say the word slowly, and think of what letter you would expect to see." Almost simultaneously, children are acquiring visual memory strategies for retrieving common words; therefore these prompts encourage them to apply their phonological and orthographic skills in flexible ways. When children are unsure of how to write a word, they try it out and think of how the word might look. Here, the teacher asks prompts

such as, "Which one looks right? How would the word look if it were written in a book?" As children build a core of known words, they use bits and pieces of these words to problem-solve on new words. The teacher prompts them to use strategies of analysis: "Is there another word you know that can help you? Do you know another word that starts like that word?" In writers' workshop, children learn to revise their spellings and to circle words that do not look right to them. They learn strategies for monitoring their spellings, trying out alternative solutions, and using resources to self-correct the words. When children acquire a repertoire of strategies for spelling words, they learn how words work.

Prompts for Solving Words	
Prompts	*Problem-Solving Task*
Say the word slowly, and listen to what you hear.	Linking sounds to letters
What can you hear first? next? last?	Sequencing of sounds to letters
Run your finger under the word. Check the word with your eyes as you say it.	Visual analysis and sequencing
What letter(s) would you expect to see in the word? Check to see if you are right.	Visual prediction and confirming strategy
Say the word in syllables. What is the first part you hear? How would you write it? What is the next part?	Linking chunks of sound to clusters of letters
Write the word several ways, and circle the one that looks right.	Strategies of comparison

Do you know another word that starts like that word? ends like that word? has a middle part like that word?	Analogy to known word or word parts

Self-Help Spelling Chart

- Say the word slowly, and listen to what you can hear.
- Write what you can hear first, next, last.
- Think of the way the word looks.
- Write the word in parts.
- Think of another word with similar parts.
- Use your practice page to try out the different spellings.
- Use classroom resources to help you.
- Ask your teacher during writing conference.

3. *Spelling instruction should consider the cognitive aspects of memory functions.* Spelling lessons should focus on a minimum of new things to learn, so as not to overload children's working memory. In designing a spelling program, there are two aspects of memory to consider:

- *Short-term memory (working memory).* This is where the brain focuses attention on specific items at a particular time; it is the place where conscious processing occurs. It involves a concentrated effort to learn pieces of information, including rehearsal and memorization techniques. The limitations of the working memory restrict the amount of information that can be remembered at a particular time. For an elementary-age child, the average capacity of working memory is five items.
- *Long-term memory.* This is where the brain organizes knowledge into an efficient network of relationships. Long-term memory is composed of patterns and experiences that are connected by a common link; thus these memories become embedded in a larger system of knowledge. Two factors play a role in long-term memory: meaning and relevance.

If children are having difficulty remembering words (a concentration task), the problem might be a lack of understanding for how words are constructed. Instead, they may be relying on short-term memory to retrieve words. Here, we are discussing a major distinction in learning to spell: a memorization task (short-term memory) versus conceptual understanding (semantic memory) that includes a network of relevant information for problem solving on new words.

Figure 4.3 illustrates how chunking visual information is a more economical and speedy process than sounding out individual letters for solving unknown words. For instance, if a child is attempting to spell the unknown word *sting*, she has two options: remember the individual letters and their associated sounds, or apply knowledge of word parts from familiar words to spell the unknown word. Research suggests that it is more efficient to attend to larger units of information for solving word problems.

4. *Children should practice spelling strategies in meaningful ways, so as to promote automaticity, transfer, and internalization.* The goal of spelling is that children will be able to spell words with accuracy and ease. Writing is a natural context for learning to spell because it provides a meaningful and communicative setting for attending to the details of words. Writing involves the brain in cross-referencing three types of perceptual data—visual, auditory, and motor—all of which are needed to produce an accurate spelling. If these sources of information are working together, they provide the

Figure 4.3 Chunking visual information is faster than sounding out individual letters.

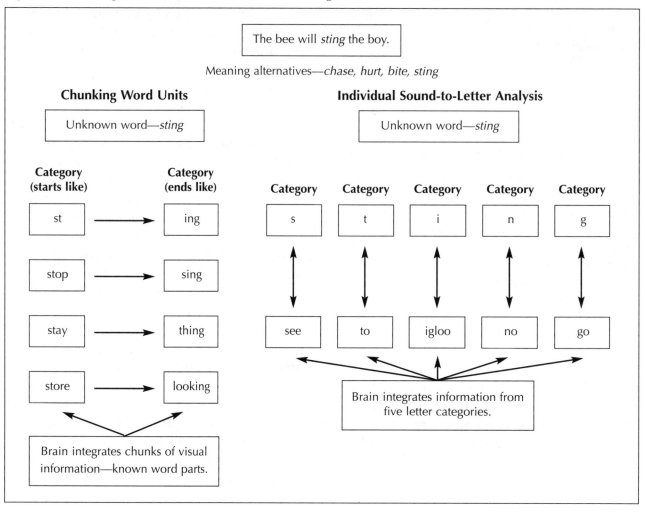

learner with feedback for confirming or rejecting the attempt. The preceding example prompts for solving words are designed to direct attention to these word-solving processes. Once children have learned how to monitor their spellings, they acquire the internal resources for linking this knowledge to other words. This process results in a well-organized network of related patterns, which serve as exemplars for spelling new words.

 5. *Self-reflection and self-correction are important goals of the good speller.* As children become more efficient word solvers, they begin to notice when their spellings do not look right. About the same time, they start using editing checklists and simple dictionaries for checking and, if necessary, self-correcting their words. Their writing samples indicate multiple attempts at spelling, and they circle the words that do not look right. Thus, children develop proofreading skills that require self-reflecting and self-correcting processes. In Figure 4.4, we can see how the student is using resources for self-checking her work.

Figure 4.4 Student self-checking her work with dictionary and spelling trial page.

6.   *Spelling lessons should recognize the social side of language.* The social side of learning occurs in two ways: teachers support children during meaningful and relevant spelling lessons; children support each other by checking and sharing their new knowledge. Children should have opportunities to interact with others about the spelling process. During spelling lessons, two activities that promote peer collaboration are word-building activities in literacy corners and the Buddy Check (Pinnell and Fountas 1998). An example of the first is a three-step process: write and check the words using the "see, say, cover, write, check" procedure; categorize the words under onset and rime patterns; and construct the words with the magnetic letters from a basket.

Buddy Check Procedure

1. Pass out one piece of paper with the spelling words and two Buddy Check sheets to each pair of students. One student will hold the spelling word sheet and be the "teacher." The other student will write on the Buddy Check sheet and be the "student."

   The "teacher" calls out the words one by one. If the "student" gets it right, she may put a check mark in the Correct column. If she gets it wrong, the "teacher" may prompt and remind the "student" of strategies she can use to figure out the word (without telling her the word). If she gets it correct the second time, she may put a check mark in the Correct column. If she does not get it correct the second time, the "teacher" tells her how to spell it, letter by letter.

   For the next round, the students switch roles and repeat the procedure.

2. Bring the whole class back together and have the students write independently on the bottom of the Buddy Check sheet how they problem-solved on one of the words. (This process will have been previously modeled by the teacher several times. The teacher can prompt to two types of words: a word that the child had difficulty with spelling, or any word that a child wants to write about.)

3. Invite two or more students to read to the class their problem-solving solutions from their Buddy Check sheets.

Spelling Instruction

Moving into Spelling Instruction

Spelling lessons provide concrete experiences that focus children's attention on the phonological and orthographic aspects of written language. The lessons in this chapter are grounded in the six beliefs of spelling acquisition, and they reflect shifts over time in the development of a spelling system. From this perspective, spelling development moves along a continuum that is aligned with the emergent, early, transitional, and fluent processing systems, described in Chapter 3. Table 4.2 outlines specific behaviors that represent children's spelling knowledge at each level of the literacy continuum. Here is a weekly spelling schedule (twenty minutes each day) from a first-grade classroom.

Table 4.2 Building Orthographic and Phonological Systems

Emergent Level	Early Level	Transitional Level	Fluent Level
Analyzes letter features; identifies letters based on discriminating features.	Letter knowledge is fast and automatic.	Letter knowledge is fast and automatic.	Letter knowledge is fast and automatic.
Semiphonetic stage of spelling; can hear and record some beginning and ending consonant sounds.	Phonetic stage of spelling; can hear and record some embedded sounds in two/three-syllable words, vowels.	Transitional spelling; attends to spelling patterns; analyzes parts of words (inflectional endings, rimes, contractions).	Mostly conventional spelling, with some transitional spelling; spells most words with minimal attention.
Knows concept of word; can construct easy words in left-to-right order (one-syllable words—*cat, can, hat, am*).	Analyzes sound sequences and letters in left-to-right order; notices interletter associations in familiar words (*th/the; sh/she*).	Uses syllable breaks to spell longer words.	Has flexible control of spelling patterns; knows when words do not look right.
Compares and classifies known words by initial sounds and basic rhyming patterns.	Uses onset and rime patterns to spell unknown words; uses known words as a base, adding inflections.	Uses more complex analogies to solve words.	Uses more complex analogies to solve words.
Sorts words according to meaning classifications; expands word knowledge by noting meaning relationships; uses a word bank.	Expands word knowledge by classification; records words in word dictionary; uses a simple dictionary.	Classifies words according to meaningful parts; uses dictionary to check spelling; uses a simple thesaurus.	Classifies words according to word meanings, including figurative and descriptive language; notices multiple meanings of words; acquires a mental dictionary of word meanings.

Weekly Spelling Schedule (Twenty Minutes per Day)

Monday
- Teacher demonstrates letter formation with one letter. She uses language prompts that describe the construction of the letter (Table 4.1).
- Children articulate the language prompts and practice writing the letter.
- Teacher introduces two new spelling words.
- Teacher models the strategy for learning the new words.
- Children practice the strategy for learning the new words.
- Teacher and children add the strategy to the self-help spelling chart.
- Children sort the words in the pocket chart by category.
- Teacher places the words in a basket for literacy corner activity.

Tuesday
- Teacher demonstrates letter formation with another letter. She uses language prompts that describe the construction of the letter.
- Children articulate the language prompts and practice writing the letter.
- Children practice writing the two words from the previous day on the dry erase board for fluency review.
- Teacher and children repeat above procedures with two new words.

Wednesday
- Teacher demonstrates letter formation with another letter. She uses language prompts that describe the construction of the letter.
- Children articulate the language prompts and practice writing the letter.
- Children practice writing the four words from the previous days on the dry erase board for fluency review.
- Teacher and children repeat procedures with two new words.

Thursday
- Children practice writing the six words from the previous days on the dry erase board for fluency review.
- Children work with partner on Buddy Check.

Friday
- Children use "see, say, cover, write, check" with this week's words.
- Teacher dictates words for spelling check.

It is important to note that the spelling block includes instruction in handwriting, for we know that automaticity with letter knowledge is critical for spelling development. (See Table 4.1 for language prompts that assist the formation of letters.)

Organizing for Spelling Instruction

Organization is a critical part of a well-managed spelling program. In a well-organized environment, children expect specific procedures and routines to be associated with a particular learning task. The predictable structure frees the minds of children so that they can focus their attention on new learning goals. We believe that children should develop self-regulatory behaviors that include organizational skills for preparing their own learning environment. Typically, children's materials include the following:

- Zipper bag to hold magnetic letters or letter cards for that day's lesson
- Counters or pennies for pushing individual sounds
- Specially prepared worksheets for analyzing sounds
- Dry erase marker and marker board
- Tissue or eraser (one teacher cut a large eraser into three parts that she gave to the children)
- Plastic basket for storing the zipper bag and marker

The teacher must also be well-organized. The teacher needs the following materials:

- Overhead projector
- Transparencies
- Magnetic letters for the day's lesson
- Dry erase marker
- Pocket chart
- Pictures from the ABC chart (see Appendix I)
- Spelling words on index cards

Selecting Words for Teaching Spelling Strategies

Our first-grade teachers have developed spelling lists that are organized according to four important overlapping and generative spelling principles:

- *Redundancy principle.* These words include commonly occurring (high-frequency) words that children read and write over and over (e.g., *am, and, it, in, is, go, the, that*)
- *Associative principle.* These words include exemplars of words with a direct letter-sound relationship. This process is taught by guiding children to say words slowly and match the individual sound with the

corresponding letter (e.g., *cat, as, can, had, mom, me, but*).

- *Directionality principle.* These words include good examples that illustrate the left-to-right sequence of sounds and letters within the word. This is first taught with one-syllable words and direct letter-sound match (e.g., *the, has, dad, did, his, with*).
- *Patterning principle.* These words include known word parts that can be used to spell new words. This is taught by associating chunks of sound to clusters of letters (e.g., *play, come, here, jumped, sing, car, girl, for, cry*).

Changes Over Time in a Primary Spelling Program

As teachers, we must observe the subtle changes that occur as children progress from being less competent to more competent spellers. Children's spelling development moves along a continuum that reflects greater control of the spelling system; they acquire knowledge that is shaped through experience and reflective practice. Gentry and Gillet (1993) describe how children go through spelling stages, beginning with the semiphonetic and ending with the conventional, or accurate, spelling stage (see also Snowball and Bolton 1999).

At the semiphonetic level, children show a budding awareness that letters are represented by sounds (generally, one or two consonant sounds are recorded for a word). At the phonetic level, this awareness becomes more refined, and children's writing reveals an understanding of letter-sound relationships within the directional sequence of a word. In the process, they begin to notice that some words contain a predictable cluster of letters that match a chunk of sound. This awareness of linguistic patterns is a necessary foundation for attending to the next spelling stage, that is, the transitional level. At this level, the "look" of a

word begins to dominate the spelling process. Here, children start to experiment with irregular spelling patterns. In the beginning stages of transitional spelling, children frequently overgeneralize their pattern knowledge, resulting in inappropriate spellings, but as they become more reflective spellers, they notice words that do not look right and their spelling becomes more conventional.

We believe that accurate spelling is the result of a cognitive process that includes attending, monitoring, searching, and self-correcting strategies (Dorn and Soffos 2001a). To illustrate this theory, we share examples of the spelling programs from several primary classrooms. In first grade, the teachers use key words as tools for teaching the children effective strategies for problem solving on words. Their spelling program is based on four levels of analysis (Table 4.3):

- *Sound analysis.* Words can be spelled by slowly articulating the sounds within the word form.
- *Visual analysis.* Some words need to be remembered by the way they look.
- *Pattern analysis.* Words consist of predictable letter sequences and patterns.
- *Analogy.* Knowledge of word parts can be used to spell unknown words.

By second grade, the children have acquired strategies for learning about words, and the spelling program is naturally embedded into the writing workshop.

First-Grade Spelling Program

Sound Analysis

In early lessons, the spelling examples include one-syllable words with two, three, or four phonemes that result in a direct letter-sound

Table 4.3 Key Words

Sound Analysis	Visual Analysis	Pattern Analysis	Analogy
am	here	day	stop (+) new = stew
at	come	play	stop (+) jump = stump
as	came	stay	me (+) house = mouse
and	have	away	be (+) all = ball
I	like	stayed	see (+) it = sit
in	little	played	me (+) heat = meat
is	my	car	for (+) sheet = feet
it	make	far	do (+) play = day
me	they	girl	the (+) ink = think
mom	there	dirt	so (+) fun = sun
can	will	hurt	then (+) why = they
cat	went	hurting	why (+) there = where
be	where	very	he (+) cow = how
but	why	funny	to (+) all = tall
big	when	cry	why (+) then = when
best	what	by	see (+) paw = saw
go	want	sky	can (+) far = car
get	was	or	sky (+) dirt = skirt
he	some	for	to (+) porch = torch
had	said	more	new (+) tight = night
has	do	store	me (+) other = mother
did	doing	porch	grow (+) seen = green
dad	to	forgot	sly (+) sheep = sleep

match. Here, the words serve as models for teaching a process of sound-to-letter analysis. Dana Autry, the teacher, introduces the lesson: "Today, we are going to learn some new words. The two new words are *am* and *at*. The first word is *am*. Watch my mouth as I say the word." Dana says the word slowly; then she encourages the children to say the word with her. She places on the overhead projector a transparency sheet that has two lines drawn in the middle of the page. The two lines represent the phonemic positions for the two sounds in the example words (*am, at*). Dana places a plastic counter below the first line; as she says the word slowly, she pushes the counter onto the first line, then the second. Dana is aware of the need to coordinate speech with action, for her goal is to help the children acquire an understanding of sound-to-letter match.

Child: I hear an *a*—like in *apple*!

Teacher: Yes, I do, too. (*Writes* a *on the first line of the transparency*.) Now, let's say *am* again slowly and listen to the next sound.

As the teacher and children slowly articulate the word, Dana pushes the counter at the overhead projector to illustrate the sound-letter match. She emphasizes the *m* sound at the end of the word while simultaneously matching her counter to the final position. One child responds, "I hear an *m*!" Dana acknowledges the child's response and links it to the key picture on the alphabet chart, "Yes, like in monkey." Then she coaches the children to blend the sounds together and check the word for its spelling from the overhead screen. "Let's say the word *am* slowly and check to see if it looks right." As the teacher and children slowly articulate the word, Dana runs her finger under the letters to match the spoken sounds. She uses explicit prompts to reinforce the action: "Do the letters match the sounds in the word? Is that the way we would spell *am*?" Then she says, "Now, I'm going to write the word *am* fast. If I forget how to write it, I will say the word slowly to help me." This simple demonstration is designed to help the children acquire an understanding of how letters and sounds work together to represent spellings.

The next step is to coach the children to apply the process to their independent work. At their seats, the children have their worksheet and plastic counters ready for practicing the new skill. The worksheet has two lines that represent the two phonemes within the word, just as the teacher's transparency model did. Dana instructs the children to place their counters under the two lines on their worksheet. Then she and the children slowly articulate the word, push the counters, identify and record the sounds, and check the word with their fingers. At the end of the interaction, the teacher reviews the process: "If you forget how to spell the word *am*, what can you do to help yourself?" The children respond, "Say it slowly!"

This brief interaction is designed to scaffold the next step in the learning cycle—the transfer of the behavior (slow articulation of sounds in sequence) to the learning of a new word (*at*). Throughout this segment, the teacher carefully observes the children and adjusts her support, as needed, to ensure that they understand the role of slow articulation for analyzing sound-to-letter sequences. At the end of the lesson, the teacher and children will add this strategy to the self-help spelling chart, which is displayed in the class for ongoing reference. During the next two days, the children will learn four new words (two each day), using the same process for analyzing sounds to letters. On Thursday, the children will use

the Buddy Check procedure to check their spellings, followed by a written explanation of their problem-solving strategies. Then, on Friday, prior to the test, the children will use the "see, say, cover, write, check" procedure. Over the next few weeks, Dana will introduce several new high-frequency words to reinforce the strategy of slow articulation and sound-to-letter analysis.

During early spelling lessons, the teacher scaffolds the children with lines drawn on paper to represent the phonemic structure of the words. However, a scaffold should be temporary—although it is often replaced by another type of scaffold. Thus, about three weeks into the program, the lines are replaced by magnetic letters (see Figure 4.5) or letter cards, and children apply the strategy of slow articulation to build letters into words.

Figure 4.5 Teacher models sound-to-letter analysis with magnetic letters.

Visual Analysis

As children learn how to analyze sounds in words, the teacher adjusts her teaching to accommodate this strategy and raises the instructional ante to a new level. Now it is time to focus the children's attention on a detailed look at words. Here, Sabrina Kessler uses words that provide good models for teaching this strategy. At the phonetic stage, the children have learned to represent a sound for a letter; now they are ready to deal with the irregularities of language, specifically, letters that are not represented by sounds. To introduce this process, Sabrina uses lines drawn on paper—this time, a line to represent each letter within a word. As before, she models the procedure at the overhead projector and uses explicit language to explain the process: "We are going to learn how to spell words by using another strategy. We've already learned to say words slowly, but some words have letters that we cannot hear. So, we need to think about how these words might look." She continues to explain: "We will use the lines to help us think about this new strategy. This time our lines are different. We have a line for every letter. When we say a word slowly, there might be a letter in the word that we can't hear." Now she presents the model word: "The first word we are going to learn today is *here*." Then Sabrina prompts the children to say the word slowly as she simultaneously runs her finger under the lines representing the letters in the word. In the process, the children acquire an understanding of the relationship between letters and sounds, and they begin to notice that some words contain additional letters to "make them look right." The following interaction illustrates the process of visual analysis:

Teacher: What letter would you expect to see first?

Child: I hear *h*—like *horse* on our chart.

Teacher: Yes, I hear an *h,* too. So, I expect to see an *h* first in this word. (*Records an* h *on the first line.*) Now, let's say *here* again and think of the letter that we would expect to see next. (*The teacher and children say the word slowly as Sabrina runs her finger slowly under the lines.*)

Child: *E*! I hear an *e*!

Teacher: Yes, I do, too. So, I would expect to see an *e* after the *h*. (*Records an* e *on the second line.*) Now, let's say the word again and think of the next letter we would expect to see. (*The teacher and children say the word slowly as Sabrina runs her finger under the lines.*)

Child: *R*!

Teacher: Yes, I would expect to see an *r,* too. (*Records it on the third line and prompts for the next letter for the fourth line.*) What do we hear next?

Child: I don't hear anything. But there's another line!

Teacher: Yes, that's because the word needs another letter to make it look right. What letter can we add to spell the word *here*?

Child: *E*! An *e* makes it spelled right!

As with all new learning, the teacher ensures that the children have the opportunity to apply the strategy to independent work at their seats. After the lesson, Sabrina coaches the children to articulate the process. "What can we write on our spelling chart to help us with words that have extra letters?" Several children respond, "Think about the way the word looks." Over the next few days, Sabrina uses exemplar words to model and reinforce the strategy of visual analysis. The lines are eliminated, and magnetic letters and letter cards are used to build words (Figures 4.6). Throughout the lessons, the teacher and children create lists of words that fit this particular category; the words are displayed on the wall as a classroom resource.

Figure 4.6 Student practices making *here* with letter cards.

Pattern Analysis

When children acquire a core of common words, the words present them with models for noticing the letter patterns. In a previous spelling lesson, the children have practiced building words from magnetic letters and letter cards. In Tonya Henderson's first-grade classroom, her spelling lessons are designed to direct children's attention to the patterns within words. She begins the lesson by activating their knowledge about rhyming patterns: "Today we are going to learn some new words. The new words are *day* and *play*. What do you know about these words?" Several children respond, "They rhyme!" Tonya praises them and prompts them to check for the visual pattern. "Yes, they do sound alike," she says. "Now, let's check to see if they also look alike."

Teacher: Put your finger under the first line on your worksheet. Say the word slowly, and run your finger under the lines.

Child: D . . . ay. I hear a *d*.
Teacher: Write the *d* above the line. Now say the word again, and think of the letter you would expect to see next.
Child: *A*!
Teacher: That's right, you can hear the *a* sound, but there is another letter that goes with the *a* to make the word look right.
Child: We need a *y*!
Teacher: That's right. Let's write the word and see if it looks right to us.

Here, Tonya prompts the children to focus their attention on the spelling pattern. She coaches them to apply their knowledge of the *ay* part to another example word in that category: "Let's try the word *play*. You have four lines on your worksheet. Say the word slowly, and think of the letters you would expect to see in the word." The children have no difficulty recording the correct spelling, and Tonya directs their attention to the pattern: "Can you hear all the letters in the word?" "No," one child says. "You can't hear the *y* at the end." Tonya explains the process: "There are many words that have letters that we cannot hear, but we need these extra letters in our spelling to make them look right." With this comment, she coaches the children to make a class list of other words with the *ay* pattern, and the list is displayed on the wall as a spelling reference. On another day, Tonya uses the same process to direct the children's attention to a new spelling pattern.

Analogy

As the children become more competent at visual analysis, the teacher designs spelling instruction that focuses almost exclusively on spelling patterns. This is an effective strategy in reading, as it enables the reader to decode unknown words at the larger unit of analysis (in contrast to sounding out individual letters—a slow process). For instance, in reading, we would expect the teacher to use prompts such as, "Is there some part of that word that you know? Do you know another word that starts or ends like that word?" This same process is utilized in writing, as children's spelling development moves from the slow articulation of sounds within a word to the fast construction of visual patterns to spell the word. In Chapter 3, we discussed the reciprocal relationship of reading, writing, and spelling; thus, our spelling lessons are designed to highlight the visual aspects of literacy learning.

A typical spelling lesson would include the manipulation of bits and pieces of known word patterns to problem-solve on unknown words—using magnetic letters, word cards, or spelling notebooks. Here is an example from a spelling lesson with Teresa Treat and her first-grade students.

Teacher: Today, we will learn a new strategy for spelling words. You will use parts of some words that you already know to help you spell some new words. Use your word cards on your desk to make the word *stop*. Now, right under *stop*, make the word *jump*. When you finish, check the words with your finger to be sure they look right.

As the children construct the words, Teresa builds the two words with magnetic letters at the overhead projector, thus providing the children with a model for checking their own work. At the same time, Teresa watches to ensure that no child is having difficulty with recalling the key words. Then, she prompts them to isolate the onset and rime parts within the two words: "Now, take away the first part of the word *stop* (the onset) and move it to the side of your desk. What part did you take away?" The children respond, "*st*!" The important lesson here is that the children must know where the linguistic break within the word structure occurs. This principle has been learned in earlier lessons that have focused on word patterns. "Now, let's take away the last part (the rime) of the word *jump* and put it beside the *st* part. Say each part and blend them together to make a new word. What word did you make?" "*Stump!*" the children exclaim. "Yes," confirms Teresa, "*stump* is a new word, but you knew some parts from other words that helped you spell it." The teacher and children apply this process to several other words, and they construct a class chart that includes a graphic of how parts of known words can be used to make new words (Figures 4.7 and 4.8). Then Teresa concludes the lesson by prompting the children to add this new strategy to the class self-help spelling chart.

Figure 4.7 Chart showing how parts of known words can be used to make new words.

Figure 4.8 Chart showing word parts.

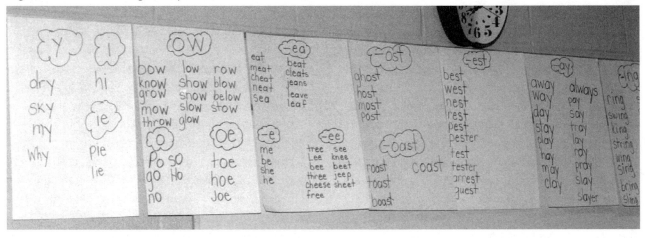

An Apprenticeship Approach to Spelling Instruction

In this section, we have shared a first-grade spelling program that includes the principles of apprenticeship learning: modeling, coaching, scaffolding, and fading. The program emphasizes a problem-solving context where children learn how to use strategies for spelling words. Although the lessons are taught during an isolated block of time, they are clearly designed to support the reading and writing processes. Thus, the teacher observes for the transfer of the spelling skills and strategies to independent reading and writing activities. As you design your spelling program, here are some important points to consider:

- Choose model words to teach a process for learning how to spell. These words become key words (or exemplars) for learning new words.
- Use one or two clear examples to model the process or strategy to the entire class.
- Coach the children to apply the skills and strategies to their independent work. Observe their behavior and scaffold them,

as needed, to ensure that they understand the process.

- Apply the particular strategy to other words. Create lists of words that fit the target category, and display these lists in the room for resources.
- Provide opportunities for the children to use this strategy in literacy corners, guided reading, and writing groups.

Second- and Third-Grade Spelling Programs

By second grade, children should have learned some efficient ways to spell words with greater accuracy. They say words slowly; they use a trial page to experiment with the "look" of words; they search for patterns within words; and they know how to use dictionaries and other resources to check and self-correct their spellings. Therefore, in second grade, spelling lessons are not a daily occurrence; rather, the teacher plans mini-lessons, as needed, to teach a particular spelling skill. However, a few children might still benefit from structured lessons, and these lessons can be presented in a small group during the morning literacy block.

At the beginning of the year, we introduce the spelling workshop to the class. It is designed to support the writing process. Here, children select words from their own writing portfolios to learn; they use a trial page to work on spellings; they confer with the teacher during writing conferences; and they create word study notebooks that categorize the words from their own writing. The process works this way:

1. Students circle words that do not look right from their writing draft. They select three to five words that they want to learn to spell.
2. Students use a trial page from their writing portfolio to attempt the spellings. First, they attempt the spelling by writing it two different ways. Then they place a check mark beside the word that does not look right. Next, they look up the word in the dictionary. If they cannot find the word, they confer with the teacher, who provides the correct spelling. They highlight the part of the word that was difficult for them in spelling.
3. Students select words from their trial pages and analyze the words according to spelling features (Figure 4.9). These words

Figure 4.10 Recording words in a word study notebook.

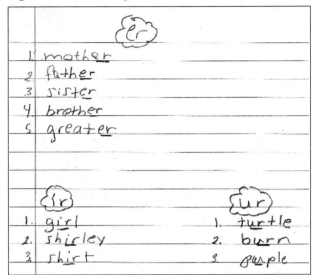

are recorded in their word study notebooks (Figure 4.10).
4. During the spelling workshop, students give these words out to each other, using a Buddy Check form.

Closing Thoughts

In this chapter, we have emphasized the development of a processing system—one that changes over time as children become self-regulated spellers. The goal of spelling is not memorization of words but a conceptual understanding of the spelling system. In the next chapter, we discuss how teachers provide students with opportunities to practice their knowledge, skills, and strategies in well-designed literacy corners, thus promoting flexibility and automaticity with known information.

Figure 4.9 Spelling trial page used to analyze words according to spelling features.

First Try	Second Try	Correct
becas	because	✓
clase	claise	clause
Shurley	Sherley	Shirley
meet	meat	meat

Teaching for
Automaticity and Transfer

A major theme of this book has been the development of a literacy processing system—one that views reading, writing, and spelling as interwoven aspects of language learning. This theory of processing implies that teachers must be able to observe changes in literacy behaviors that indicate changes in cognitive control (see Figure 1.3, which displays the movement from awareness to self-regulation). In Chapter 3, we shared charts of typical literacy behaviors at emergent, early, transitional, and fluent processing levels. This guide provides teachers with a scaffold for observing specific literacy behaviors along a processing continuum. The important point is that the only way we can infer a movement to higher-level cognitive processing is to observe behavioral changes in a student's response to a learning task. In our work with teachers, we ask questions such as

What is the child noticing?
Do you see a change in how quickly the child
    responds to a problem-solving task?
Is the processing time becoming faster?
Does the child show greater control today
    than yesterday?

Is the child able to apply the knowledge,
    skills, and strategies to different contexts and for different purposes?
How do you predict the child will respond
    on a similar task tomorrow?

The ultimate goal of teaching is the development of a self-regulated learner—a student with the capacity to guide and monitor his own learning on different tasks and for different purposes. This implies that students must be able to apply knowledge gained from assisted activities to independent work. Furthermore, it means that teachers must create conditions that promote the transfer of knowledge across changing contexts. How does the curriculum play a role in promoting automaticity and flexibility of knowledge? In this chapter, we discuss how teachers create opportunities at literacy corners for students to use what they already know to solve problems in related areas (see Figures 2.2 and 2.3). What is the theory (or purpose) behind the literacy corners? How do teachers organize corner activities for productive learning? Where does writing fit into the corner activities? How do the tasks support the development of a literacy processing system? These questions serve as a framework for our discussion of literacy corner activities.

The Theory Behind Literacy Corners

In our classroom experiences, we have found that many teachers perceive literacy corners (or centers) as a management technique to keep children busy while the teacher works with small groups. Although this is a positive outcome of a literacy corner, this is *not* the reason for using them. Instead, from a cognitive perspective, well-designed literacy tasks provide students with opportunities to transfer knowledge gained from assisted activities to independent contexts. Let's look at two important theories that support the role of independent literacy tasks in the development of a literacy processing system:

- *Sustained attention*. This is an important theory that relates to self-regulation. A common characteristic of struggling readers is the inefficient and haphazard way they attend to tasks. These students show a poor pattern of monitoring and sustaining attention toward the completion of a particular goal; they are easily distracted, lack motivation, and are unsure of what they know. How do students develop the ability to maintain attention for a prolonged period of time? Sustained attention is shaped through meaningful and relevant opportunities where students learn *how* to use their own knowledge to solve similar problems in different contexts. Specially designed tasks (based on reading and writing knowledge) enable students to apply their current strategies for successfully completing a new task.

- *Automaticity and flexibility*. This theory is critical for higher-level literacy development, as it implies that knowledge moves from the overt to the covert level (the subroutine level) with successful practice over a prolonged period of time. Recall that in Chapter 1 we discussed how children first attend to new learning at a very conscious level of attention, but eventually this knowledge goes underground, freeing children's attention to notice new things. Here, the student's old knowledge serves as a basis for interpreting new knowledge and experience. This dynamic interplay of old and new knowledge serves to build cognitive control. What does this have to do with literacy tasks at corners? Simply put, children *must* have opportunities to practice (and overlearn) their knowledge in different ways so that important information and strategies become automatic (unconscious) reactions of the brain. For early readers and writers, a solid core of known information furnishes them with visual tools for problem solving within continuous text. This level of internal control provides students with the capacity to guide and monitor their learning to new and higher planes.

These theories imply that literacy corners are mostly designed for early readers and writers. When students have learned how to sustain their attention on problem-solving tasks for a prolonged period of time, they possess the ability to attend to longer and more complex texts. Generally, by second grade, students do not need the full range of literacy corners. However, we realize that struggling readers and writers can be found at all grade levels; thus, literacy corner activities should be designed to meet the individual needs of all students. As teachers, it will serve us well to keep in mind the cognitive aspects of learning as well as the organizational and management techniques of teaching.

Organizing for Independence with Literacy Corners

An important principle of apprenticeship learning is the role of routine in promoting literacy development. Teachers must create well-organized learning environments encompassing familiar routines that promote children's independence. Children should participate in planning, rehearsing, and organizing the learning structure of the classroom. In doing this, they acquire important organizational skills that are directly linked to self-regulation (Dorn, French, and Jones 1998). In organizing for literacy corners, we use the following guidelines to create literacy tasks that engage children in productive learning:

- A literacy task must promote problem-solving strategies that are based on what children already know. Teachers collect ongoing documentation from running records, writing samples, and classroom observations to plan for problem-solving opportunities at literacy corners.
- A literacy task is first introduced in an assisted situation with guidance and coaching from the teacher. The teacher ensures that the students understand the goal of the task and the specific instructions for carrying it out. (Later, we share examples of how Carla introduces literacy task cards to her students.)
- A literacy task is designed to support a student's reading and writing development. All word-building activities are based on a developmental continuum of processing behaviors at emergent, early,

and transitional reading levels (see Chapter 3).

- Each literacy task includes a writing component: the student records his or her thinking process in a special notebook. In some classrooms, teachers use a "traveling corner log" that contains all the corner activities for the year. In other classrooms, teachers prefer that students have a separate log at each corner.

Recall in Chapter 2 that the students work in literacy corners while the teacher meets with small groups of students for guided reading and assisted writing. Based on this schedule, students must be able to work independently in the literacy corners for approximately one hour. As we stated earlier, students must be able to sustain their attention on problem-solving tasks for a prolonged period of time. Thus, literacy corners remain "under construction" until children are ready to use them in a productive manner. In Chapter 1, we explained how the rules and guidelines for using literacy corners are discussed with the students prior to the opening of any corner. When a teacher feels that students are ready to learn from the corner activities, this literacy corner is opened. The appropriateness of the literacy task cards at each corner plays a critical role in the children's learning.

The following literacy corners provide students with valuable learning experiences that link problem-solving strategies across the curriculum.

Math Corner

In the math corner, specific task cards are designed to promote problem-solving strategies that link to reading and writing processes (Figure 5.1). This corner includes activities that are based on a student's actual level of devel-

Figure 5.1 Task cards at math corner.

Figure 5.2 Classroom post office corner.

opment. Students record their thinking in a literacy log.

Rhythm and Rhyme Corner

This corner contains a collection of familiar poems from shared reading and spelling events. Students use highlighter tape and markers to spotlight words; they use magnetic letters to construct and deconstruct words; they classify letter groups according to common patterns; and they record this information in their literacy logs.

Post Office Corner

Students write letters to other students, teachers, and parents. The classroom post office shown in Figure 5.2 is designed with mail cubbies for each student.

Writing Corner

The writing corner is equipped with writing tools, including checklists, topic lists, writing guidelines, dictionaries, thesauruses, staplers, publishing materials, and other resources for independent writing. Here, a student can continue working on a writing piece from writers'

workshop or begin a new topic based on ideas that are displayed in this corner.

Spelling Corner

The spelling tasks provide students with opportunities to work with their spelling words over time. Special task cards are created to reinforce spelling knowledge in flexible ways (Figure 5.3).

Name Corner

Students' names provide them with personal opportunities to learn about print, including beginning and ending sounds, syllable breaks,

Figure 5.3 Task cards at spelling corner.

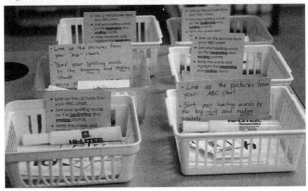

Figure 5.4 Name corner.

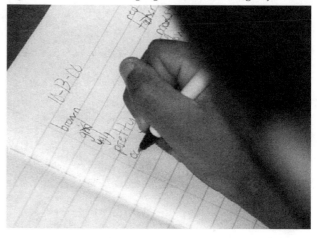

Figure 5.5 Student in language corner recording adjectives.

rhyming patterns, digraphs and blends, and vowel patterns. Figure 5.4 shows how a name corner is set up. Appendix J gives examples that teachers can use to create name task cards.

Language Corner

In this corner, children continue to learn about words and how they are used in the meaning-making process. During writers' workshop, teachers use mini-lessons that focus on language skills, and students monitor their writing for strong action words and describing words. This skill is reinforced in the language corner, where task cards focus on the categorization of nouns, verbs, adjectives, and adverbs. Figure 5.5 shows a student just completing a task card for recording adjectives in his literacy log. We can see how he has monitored his attempts by crossing out three nouns from his list.

ABC Corner

This corner is used mostly for kindergarten and first-grade students. The purpose is to support emergent and early readers' attention to print. Activities in this corner include sorting and categorizing letters; linking letters to sounds; reading ABC books and charts; form-

ing letters with a variety of materials; making alphabet books; categorizing words according to first letter; building high-frequency words; reading word cards; and making vocabulary books. As with all corner activities, students record their learning in a literacy log.

Science Corner

This corner contains a range of informational books on topics that relate to class discussions (Figure 5.6). Also, materials for conducting experiments and other hands-on activities are

Figure 5.6 Science corner.

Figure 5.7 Student science entry in literacy log.

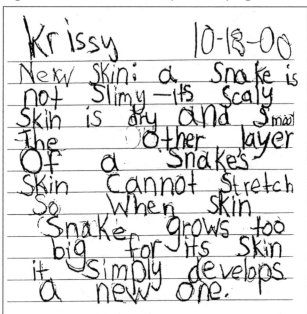

> Krissy   10-18-00
> New skin: a snake is
> not slimy—its scaly
> skin is dry and small
> The   other layer
> of   a   snake's
> skin cannot stretch
> so   when skin
> snake grows too
> big for its skin
> it simply develops
> a new one.

housed in this corner. Students record their learning in their literacy logs (Figure 5.7).

Reading Corner

This corner contains a range of reading materials, including familiar reading baskets, browsing books, and read-alouds. This corner allows students to practice successful reading practices and to read for enjoyment.

Word-Building Corner

This corner is designed to present children with word-building opportunities that are aligned with their guided reading groups. Individual baskets—with all materials for completing literacy tasks—are displayed together on a designated shelf. This organizational format allows children to remove the basket from an appropriate place. Because of flexible grouping for guided reading, the children might work from baskets on different

shelves. The important point is that the students are presented with tasks that are specially created to support their reading and writing development.

In this section, we've described typical literacy corners that play an important part in promoting students' transfer of knowledge across changing conditions. Each corner includes specific literacy tasks that are based on students' learning from assisted lessons with the teacher. Independent reading and writing tasks are embedded in all corners, specifically, the reading and writing corners that focus entirely on continuous texts. Here, we need to make an important point. *It is expected that all students use the reading and writing corners every day; we believe that practice in whole texts is the basis of self-regulated learning.*

We now focus our discussion exclusively on the literacy tasks at the word-building corner. We have found that this corner can present the greatest challenge for teachers in planning productive activities that support the development of a processing system. An important question to ask is, How do the literacy tasks relate to the development of a self-regulated literacy system?

Literacy Task Cards at Word-Building Corner

At the word-building corner, we provide students with specially designed literacy tasks that support the acquisition of word knowledge at the emergent, early, and transitional reading levels. The task cards are placed in baskets, and students work independently on specific tasks that are aimed at their actual level of development (recall Vygotsky's learning zones from Chapter 1). Although each child is working on an individualized task, the teacher groups a slightly higher-performing child at the corner with a child who might need some additional assistance.

The goal of the literacy task is to support the development of the reading, writing, and spelling systems. In Chapter 3, we discussed how a literacy processing system develops over time. We described how the literacy behaviors of students become more refined and automatic as they acquire greater competence on a particular task. We talked about the importance of small-group lessons (both guided reading and assisted writing) for scaffolding students in their zone of proximal development. Now, we discuss the reciprocal relationship between the three literacy systems to specific literacy tasks that are placed in the word-building corner. We'll look at these theories in terms of observable behaviors that we would expect to see as students acquire strategies for word solving (Table 5.1).

- *Reading system (decoding and reading fluency).* The reader must learn how to self-monitor using known information (letters, words, and word parts). He must decode unknown words at larger units of analysis. As his word-solving skills become more sophisticated, he reads most words fluently and automatically. Also, he acquires meanings for words and uses this knowledge to solve unknown words.
- *Writing system (encoding and writing fluency).* The writer must transcribe words fluently. He acquires efficient strategies for recording words according to chunks of sound and visual patterns. He recognizes when words do not look right and uses resources to check and self-correct spellings. As he acquires more experience with words, his vocabulary knowledge increases and he revises word choices at the meaning level.

- *Spelling system (encoding and spelling fluency).* The speller must learn how words work. She uses information about known words and word parts to solve unknown words. She applies a flexible range of strategies for spelling words. As she accumulates more experiences with reading and writing, her vocabulary knowledge expands, and she uses this information to attend to word meanings.
- *Literacy task cards (automaticity and transfer).* The goal of the task cards is to provide students with an opportunity to apply their word-solving strategies to independent work. In the process, they acquire flexibility and automaticity with known information. Because of the special nature of the task cards and their link to the language systems, students learn how to transfer their knowledge to a new context. Here, problem-solving activities require them to sort words according to structural and meaningful categories.

From our perspective, a literacy processing system is grounded in a cognitive model that emphasizes reciprocal connections across literacy tasks. This is in contrast to a curriculum that presents language opportunities in fragmented and isolated parts. In support of this theory, we've identified six concepts that are embedded in reading, writing, and spelling processes. The ultimate goal of all teaching is that our students will become independent and self-regulated learners. Toward this goal, Teresa, Carla, and I have constructed a set of literacy task cards (Dorn, Soffos, and Treat 2001; Dorn and Soffos 2001a) that are aligned with the three language processes. To illustrate the reciprocal nature of the language tasks, we'll discuss one example—becoming aware of the print-sound code—as it relates to the three language systems. Then we encourage you to

Table 5.1 A Reciprocal Framework for Learning About Words

Reading System	Writing System	Spelling System	Task Cards
Decoding and Reading Fluency	***Encoding and Writing Fluency***	***Encoding and Spelling Fluency***	***Automaticity and Transfer***
Monitor text using known information; decode unknown words at larger units of analysis; read most words fluently and automatically; attend to word meanings.	Transcribe words fluently; use knowledge of word patterns to write unknown words; recognize when words do not look right and use resources to check and correct spellings; revise word choices at meaning level.	Learn how words work; use information about known words and word parts to solve unknown words; apply flexible strategies for spelling words; expand vocabulary; attend to word meanings.	Apply word knowledge to independent task; acquire flexibility and automaticity with known information; promote transfer of knowledge; sort words according to structural and meaning cues.
Becoming Aware of Print-Sound Code	***Becoming Aware of Print-Sound Code***	***Becoming Aware of Print-Sound Code***	***Practicing Print-Sound Strategies***
Read high-frequency words with ease; use first letter and last letter to monitor word boundaries; articulate first letter to initiate checking action on unknown word; attend to some endings.	Write high-frequency words with ease; say words slowly and match sound to letter in single-syllable words; compose one-, two-, and three-sentence stories.	Slow articulation; hear and record sounds in sequence (one-syllable words).	Practice word construction with high-frequency words; apply left-to-right sequence of letter-to-sound match; sort known words according to first letter category; sort words according to concept category.
Increasing Awareness of Print-Sound Code	***Increasing Awareness of Print-Sound Code***	***Increasing Awareness of Print-Sound Code***	***Practicing Print-Sound Strategies***
Expand high-frequency word knowledge; use known letters and sounds to begin searching through word; control 1–1 matching on two- and three-syllable words; attend to digraph patterns.	Write high-frequency words with ease; hear and record some embedded sounds; use some pattern knowledge from known words to help with unknown words; compose longer messages.	Slow articulation; hear and record sounds in sequence; attend to how some words look; hear syllable breaks in two- and three-syllable words; attend to digraphs from known words.	Practice word control by building known words and sorting by first letter, middle letter, and ending letters; sort some words by known digraph patterns (*th/the, sh/she*).
Gaining Control of the Print-Sound System	***Gaining Control of the Print-Sound System***	***Gaining Control of the Print-Sound System***	***Practicing Print-Sound Strategies***
Search through words in serial order and blend letters to sounds; attend to word endings.	Show greater ease in linking sounds to letters from beginning to ending sequence; attend to endings.	Take known words and add known endings to make new words (*ing, s, ed, er*).	Take known words and add known endings to the ends of words to make new words.
Developing Control of the Print-Sound Code	***Developing Control of the Print-Sound Code***	***Developing Control of Print-Sound Code***	***Practicing Print-Sound Strategies***
Take words apart at larger units of visual analysis; analyze some words by meaning components.	Record words with greater ease; analyze larger units of sounds to letters for recording unknown words.	Analyze words according to commonly occurring spelling patterns, contractions, and compound words.	Sort words by commonly occurring spelling patterns; match contractions and compounds to meaningful parts; record "sorted" words and highlight patterns in word study books.

Table 5.1 A Reciprocal Framework for Learning About Words *(continued)*

Reading System	Writing System	Spelling System	Task Cards
Extending Control of the Print-Sound Code	*Extending Control of the Print-Sound Code*	*Extending Control of the Print-Sound Code*	*Practicing Print-Sound Strategies*
Take words apart with greater ease during reading; attend to visual patterns and use known parts to solve unknown words.	Write words with greater fluency; use parts of known words to construct unknown words; compose longer messages with more complex sentence structures and vocabulary.	Apply analogies by using parts of known words to solve unknown words; manipulate onset and rime patterns to make new words.	Practice using parts of known words to read and write unknown words; record words, highlight parts, and describe problem-solving actions in word study notebook.
Enlarging the System	*Enlarging the System*	*Enlarging the System*	*Enlarging the System*
Apply knowledge of meaningful parts to unknown words; expand vocabulary knowledge.	Use new vocabulary in writing stories; apply knowledge of meaningful units to analyze words.	Use parts of words (prefixes, suffixes) to spell unknown words (meaning patterns).	Categorize words by meaning parts; record and highlight word in word study notebook; describe process.

link the six concepts to the emergent, early, transitional, and fluent processing charts that we've described in Chapter 3.

Under concept 1 of the reading system, children acquire a basic core of high-frequency words as they encounter these words repeatedly in familiar and new texts. Also, the students learn to attend to first-letter cues as a visual source for initiating a response to unknown words. During the writing event, children have additional opportunities to practice fluent control of high-frequency words and to analyze the sounds within unknown words. As their stories become longer, the opportunities to learn about print are increased. Under concept 1 of the spelling system, young learners apply strategies of slow articulation and hearing and recording sounds in sequence. This strategy represents a process of analyzing sound-to-letter relationships (i.e., the sound is pronounced first, then the letter is matched to the corresponding sound). Now, recall that in Chapter 4 we discussed how the teacher uses clear models and exemplar words (e.g., one-syllable words with exact letter-to-sound

matches) to direct children's attention to the strategy of sound-to-letter analysis. During reading events, the process is reversed, with the learner perceiving the letter first, then attaching the corresponding sound to the perceived letter. This reciprocal process (sound-to-letter and letter-to-sound) is taught through flexible opportunities that allow children to apply analytical strategies across both reading and writing events. In building a self-regulated literacy system, children must learn the transferability of their problem-solving strategies to different contexts. Under concept 1, the literacy tasks are aligned with the three language systems, thus providing children with reinforcement experiences in related areas. For instance, the specific directions on the cards instruct students to build high-frequency words and to sort known words according to first-letter categories. Here, the important point is that children must understand how knowledge can be self-generated to different contexts; thus, through successful practice, the learning becomes automatic, a routine that no longer requires conscious attention.

In our work with classroom teachers, we've used Table 5.1 and the processing charts from Chapter 3 to plan appropriate word-building activities for literacy corners. We encourage you to study all six concepts and relate them to your work with young learners. To further illustrate our point, let's discuss the link between guided reading levels and specific literacy tasks.

The Emergent Level

Problem Solving

The goal of the emergent level is to promote students' attention to print. Here, literacy tasks provide children with opportunities to hear sounds within words and to sequence the letters in some known words. Near the end of the emergent level, some behaviors that indicate students' control of the print-sound code are the following:

- Attend to print using some known letters or words.
- Point to words in a one-to-one match throughout one to three lines of patterned texts.
- Recognize the link between known letters and related sounds.
- Acquire an understanding of left-to-right directional movement.
- Fluently read some high-frequency words in easy texts.
- Analyze letter features and identify letters based on discriminating features.
- Acquire concept of word and construct single-syllable words in a left-right order.
- Notice relationships between known letters and sounds as they relate to special key words.
- Compare and categorize words by initial sounds and basic rhyming patterns.

The literacy task cards are designed so that students can practice these behaviors on independent tasks.

Introducing the Literacy Task Cards

In small-group settings, teachers assist children in performing literacy tasks that are supportive of their guided reading levels. At the emergent level, students are reading simple patterned books with high picture support and large spaces between words (see Chapters 2 and 3). In the following example, Carla introduces a literacy task card to a group of emergent readers. The specific task is to guide students in matching letters to sounds in one-syllable words. The materials for this task include six picture cards (*cat, sun, man, hat, hen, fox*), magnetic letters for constructing each word, and students' literacy logs for recording the words.

Carla begins by directing the students' attention to specific strategies she has observed during their interactive writing group: "Boys and girls, I've noticed in your writing that when you come to words you don't know how to spell, you say the words slowly and listen to the sounds. I've also noticed that you use your ABC chart to help you when you can't remember the letter for that sound, or when you can't remember how to write the letter." Then she establishes the purpose of the lesson: "You can use these same strategies in your word-building corner." She pulls out the literacy task card and all materials. "I have prepared a literacy task card, some picture cards, and some magnetic letters for you to practice saying words slowly and building the words with magnetic letters." Then Carla holds up the card and says, "Let's read the task card." As she reads the directions, she coaches the children to apply the steps in order. She believes that with successful practice the children will quickly internalize the steps for independently carrying out the tasks. This process is mediated through simple steps and redundant directions that reappear in many of the literacy tasks. The steps for this particular literacy task include

- Choose a picture.
- Say the word slowly.
- Build the word with magnetic letters.
- Write the word, saying it slowly as you write it.

"The first step is to line up your picture cards," Carla instructs the children. Then she passes out the picture cards, and together they discuss the picture names. Next, she lines up the magnetic letters on a small magnetic board, exactly like the boards in the word-building corner. "Ricky," she says, "tell us the name of your picture card." She asks other children to identify their picture cards because she knows that the success of the task will depend on their ability to use the right words for the pictures. As Ricky identifies the picture for *hen*, Carla guides the students to say the word slowly. Next, Carla coaches the children to construct the word with their magnetic letters. "Say the word as you make it with your magnetic letters." The process continues with Carla coaching and scaffolding the children as they complete the literacy task. As the session ends, Carla models for the children how to record the words in their literacy logs. Then she says, "Now that you know how to do the task, I'll place the basket in your word-building corner and you can practice making words all by yourself."

The Early Level

Problem Solving

At the early level, students monitor their reading with greater ease, and as a result, they engage in more efficient searching behaviors to solve problems within text. Near the end of the early level, children have begun to notice the spelling patterns within words. Some behaviors that indicate students' control of the print-sound code are the following:

- Use known words and patterns to check on reading.
- Search through words in a left-to-right sequence and blend letters into sounds.
- Take words apart at the larger unit of analysis.
- Read high-frequency words fast, fluently, and automatically.
- Become faster at noticing errors, and initiate multiple attempts to self-correct.
- Spell most unknown words phonetically, including embedded sounds in two- and three-syllable words.
- Notice relationships between letter patterns and clusters of sound.
- Use known words as a base for adding inflections.
- Use known words and patterns to build unknown words.
- Manipulate letters to form simple analogies.

At this level, the literacy task cards are designed to support students as they move from phonetic spelling to transitional spelling. For instance, at the lower end of the early continuum, students are required to match letters and sounds in sequence. Near the end of the early continuum, students have acquired an awareness of spelling patterns.

Introducing the Literacy Task Cards

At the early level, the introduction to the task card is adjusted to accommodate students' increasing control of visual information. Here, Carla introduces a task card that focuses on vowel patterns, in this case, *oy* and *oi* patterns.

She begins by describing her observations of children's writing behaviors: "Boys and girls, I've noticed that when you are writing words in your stories that you are thinking about the way words look. So, I've prepared for you a new task so that you can practice the strategy in your word-building corner." Carla pulls out a new task basket that contains all the materials needed to complete the task. The task directions are as follows:

- Line up the category cards (*oi–oy*).
- Choose a picture card.
- Match the word under the picture card.
- Sort the word according to the vowel pattern (*oi–oy*).
- Write the word in your notebook.
- Highlight the vowel pattern.

Carla points to the first bullet on the task card and reads it with the children. Sam lines up the category cards on the floor in front of the students. Carla reminds them, "When you hear the *oy* sound, you can expect to see it spelled with either 'oi' or 'oy'. You have to think about which spelling makes the word look right." "Yes," comments Stacy. "It's like when we write the word both ways on our practice page in writing." Carla validates Stacy's response. As she reads the next bullet, she passes out the picture cards. She follows this process as she goes through each bullet—modeling, coaching, and scaffolding the students in completing the literacy task. Then she says, "Now that you know how to complete this task, I'll place it in your word-building corner, and you can practice it when you go there."

The Transitional Level

Problem Solving

At the transitional level, students have developed a range of flexible strategies for working on text. Their decoding skills are more sophisticated and refined; thus they read longer texts with greater accuracy and fluency. They take words apart on the run when reading, and they use word meanings to solve unknown words. Some behaviors that indicate the students' control of the print-sound code are the following:

- Solve multisyllabic words by noticing parts within the words.
- Quickly take words apart on the run while reading.
- Read longer texts with greater accuracy and fluency.
- Use word meanings to solve word problems (prefixes, suffixes, roots, and compound words).
- Analyze unknown words with greater efficiency and speed.
- Use syllable breaks to spell longer words.
- Use more complex analogies to analyze words.
- Analyze parts of words (e.g., inflectional endings, rimes, and contractions).
- Spell words with greater accuracy.
- Show evidence of transitional spelling for words with more unusual patterns.

At this level, the literacy task cards are designed to support students in applying visual analysis strategies.

Introducing the Literacy Task Cards

At this level, students understand how to analyze words according to visual patterns. In this example of a transitional task, Carla introduces the students to the task of "taking words apart." She begins with a standard introduction: "Boys and girls, I have noticed that in your reading you are taking words apart using word parts. Also, in your writing, you are writing words faster because you are spelling them in parts. So, let's look at our task card for the word-building corner that can help us practice this strategy." The task directions are as follows:

- Choose a picture card.
- Make the word with magnetic letters.
- Read and write the words in your notebook.
- Draw lines to show how you took the word apart.

Carla pulls out the basket and asks Karen to prepare the cards and letters for working on the task. Karen lines up the pictures and magnetic letters on the floor. Carla hands the task card to Heather and asks her to read the first bullet on the card. As Heather reads the directions, Carla passes out the picture cards to the students and they discuss the picture names. Then Heather reads the next bullet and the students use the magnetic letters to build the word in parts. The process continues until the task is completed, and then the basket is added to the corner for practice.

Task Requirements and Built-in Scaffolds

It is important for young learners to practice skills and strategies in multiple contexts, thus gaining a deeper understanding of their own knowledge. The challenge for teachers is to create constructive problem-solving opportunities that are matched to children's literacy levels. In designing literacy tasks, we've considered the developmental nature of each task at three levels of reading control (emergent, early, transitional). Although the overall goal for each level remains constant (recall the theories of scaffolding from Chapter 1), the task requirements at each level are adjusted to accommodate the

student's knowledge from a previous level. Let's look at two examples that illustrate the theory behind the literacy task cards: rhyming words and syllable breaks.

Rhyming Words

At the emergent level, the students are learning how to listen to rhyming patterns (in the absence of print). Here, the materials include pictures only, and the students are required to match the rhyming pictures (Figure 5.8):

Materials

- Fourteen picture cards.

Tasks

- Line up the pictures.
- Match the pictures that rhyme.

For emergent readers, it is important to introduce this task in a small-group setting, so that the teacher can coach and scaffold students in task directions and accurate identification of pictures.

Figure 5.8 Rhyming tasks for emergent readers.

At the early level, the task requirements are adjusted to reflect students' attention to the printed word (Figure 5.9):

Materials

- Fourteen picture cards.
- Fourteen word cards that match the pictures.

Tasks

- Match the rhyming words to the pictures.
- Do they sound alike and look alike?
- Write the words in your notebook.
- Highlight the rhyming part of the word.

Here, the task is modified to include new knowledge. For instance, students are now required to match the word and picture according to sound patterns. Also, a new requirement is introduced into the task difficulty: Do the words sound alike and look alike? At this

Figure 5.9 Rhyming task for early readers.

point, students are learning to attend to visual patterns, yet the process is scaffolded by ensuring that the words fit the "sound alike" pattern only. Furthermore, attention to patterns is reinforced as the children are required to record the words in their literacy logs and highlight the rhyming part of each word.

At the transitional level, the scaffolding is adjusted once again; at this level, students have acquired more sophisticated strategies of visual analysis. They are reading at higher text levels, and they've learned how to take words apart with greater efficiency. For transitional readers, the materials and tasks are as follows:

Materials

- Twelve picture cards.
- Twelve word cards that match the pictures.
- Two category cards.

Tasks

- Match the rhyming words to the pictures.
- Do they sound alike and look alike?
- Sort the words.
- Read and write the sorted rhyming words.

Sorting has been added to the task requirements; the children sort and record the words under two categories. Then they write the words in their word study notebook.

Syllable Breaks

In this example, we apply the process of scaffolding to the learning of syllable breaks. Table 5.2 shows the syllable break tasks for emergent and early readers. At the emergent level, students listen to the larger breaks in a word and match the pictures to category cards of one and two syllables. At the early level, the task requirements are adjusted to include print knowledge, and students record the words in

Table 5.2 Syllable Break Tasks for Emergent and Early Readers

Emergent Readers	Early Readers
Materials	*Materials*
• Six picture cards. • Category cards for one and two syllables.	• Five picture cards. • Five word cards. • Category cards for one, two, and three syllables.
Tasks	*Tasks*
• Choose a picture. • Clap the syllables. • Place the picture in the correct category by number of syllables.	• Choose a picture. • Clap the syllables. • Place the picture in the correct category by number of syllables. • Match the words to the pictures. • Read the words, and write them in your notebook.

their word study notebooks under the appropriate categories.

At the transitional level, one of the syllable break tasks is to use lines to separate the word into syllable breaks (Figure 5.10).

Figure 5.10 Syllable break tasks for transitional readers.

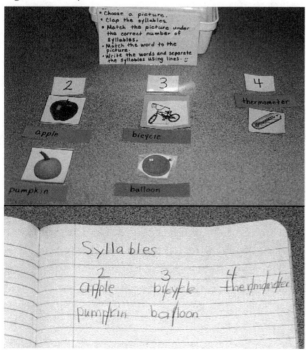

Materials

- Seven picture cards.
- Seven word cards.
- Category cards for one, two, and three syllables.

Tasks

- Choose a picture.
- Match the words to the pictures.
- Clap the syllables.
- Sort the words and pictures into the correct categories by number of syllables.
- Write the words, and use lines to separate each word into syllables.

These examples can serve as models for helping teachers construct literacy tasks that are grounded in a cognitive model of learning, specifically, changes that occur over time in the development of orthographic and phonological knowledge. We encourage teachers to work together in studying behaviors that indicate how children are problem solving on a range of literacy tasks.

Closing Thoughts

In this chapter, we have discussed an important concept in higher-level learning, that is, the theory of automaticity and transfer. This theory is critical in shaping a processing system. In the first four chapters, we discussed how teachers coach and scaffold children during small-group, whole-group, and individual conferences. In this chapter, we focused our attention on the need for productive and constructive learning activities that facilitate the transfer of knowledge. Moreover, an important goal of processing theory is the development of automatic control of knowledge, thus freeing the attention to focus on new learning. The task cards at literacy corners are designed to enable students to apply their knowledge, skills, and strategies across changing circumstances. This theory implies that students will develop self-regulatory behaviors, that is, the capacity to monitor, guide, and regulate their learning in flexible and generative ways. In the final chapter, we apply the theories of self-regulation to our work with teachers.

6

Developing Self-Regulated Teachers

In previous chapters, we focused on the relationship between teaching and learning, specifically, how teachers design instructional conditions that provide children with problem-solving opportunities. Can the principles of apprenticeship literacy be applied to the professional development of teachers? In this chapter, we share stories from teachers who've used apprenticeship techniques—modeling, coaching, scaffolding, and fading—to learn new tasks. Moreover, we give examples from classrooms where model teachers serve as mentors for novice teachers who are taking on the new learning. How can teachers design, within the course of a normal day, a professional context that allows for collaboration and problem-solving opportunities? Do the theories of self-regulation, problem solving, and transfer apply to the professional climate of teaching? These are questions that guide our discussion.

A Context for Promoting Change

What leads to changes in teacher beliefs and instructional practices? Let's begin with this assumption: true change is an internal process that reflects a mental reorganization of our perceptions and knowledge. Also, this internal reorganization is shaped through observations and experiences that might challenge our existing assumptions, thus causing us to reevaluate our old beliefs in the context of new information. Here, meaningfulness and relevance are critical aspects of the change process. Yet, is it possible that relevance might be more important than meaning? If we cannot perceive the relationship of the new learning to our own teaching, then it is unlikely that we will apply it. So, how do we promote conditions of relevance? Simply put, relevance is personal—based on a unique set of perceptions, interpretations, and experiences—thus, *it cannot be imposed on a learner.* How do we create a context where teachers begin to notice the relevance of a new curriculum for influencing their teaching of children? To answer this question, we briefly revisit the discussion of the learning process from previous chapters.

Recall that in Chapter 1 we discussed the need for children to have clear models that enable them to interpret the teacher's prompts and to self-monitor their own learning. Then we stressed the importance of good models for presenting students with a standard for comparing and assessing their own progress. Without a model, the teaching goal becomes abstract and difficult to conceptualize. Furthermore, even with a model, the interpretations of the concept will be shaped by the experiences of the learner. Now, this means that the learning will occur at different rates and along different paths. It also implies that a more knowledgeable person—in our case, the teacher—will coach and scaffold the learner along the way. In this context, the social and cognitive processes work together to shape the development of new theories and practices.

In our work with classroom teachers, we've come to realize that a well-designed model is a critical piece for visualizing a new concept. For instance, if we expect teachers to implement a curriculum for literacy, we need to provide teachers with a model for how this process works in a typical primary classroom. Can you remember a time when you attended a workshop and later tried to implement some of the ideas in your classroom? Too often, good ideas were abandoned simply because we needed more support in the implementation process. In this chapter, we share how teachers have created model classrooms as learning labs for observing, coaching, and scaffolding other teachers as they implement literacy changes in their own classrooms. Laura McKinney, a literacy coach at a high-poverty school in Blytheville, Arkansas, notes how model classrooms play a critical role in the change process: "When teachers observe students—like their own students—making unusual progress, their interest is piqued. The elements of change creep under the doors of other classrooms, and teachers begin to rethink their own theories of how children learn."

Apprenticeships in Teaching

The first step in promoting change is a desire to change, which is generally mediated by a teacher's frustration with students' progress. Here, we believe that change can be accelerated if we create apprenticeship-type conditions where more experienced teachers coach and mentor other teachers as they take on new learning. The goal is a self-regulated teacher who recognizes the capacity of her knowledge for guiding, monitoring, and reflecting on her own progress. This is the same goal that we have for the students we teach, that is, the development of self-regulated learners. We have applied the principles of apprenticeship learning to a range of literacy contexts for young children (Dorn, French, and Jones 1998). The same principles are the foundation for our work with classroom teachers. Here, we continue to link these principles to the professional context of the teaching environment.

Observation and Responsive Teaching

Teachers schedule time to observe other teachers as they teach specific literacy components. Preconferences are held to formulate observational questions and discuss expectations for students' learning. Postconferences are held to discuss the influence of teaching opportunities on students' learning behaviors. Teachers are guided in how to take observational notes, ask questions, keep reflective logs, and summarize their notes according to teaching and learning patterns. Figure 6.1 shows Linda Wilsey and Sabrina Kessler discussing their notes from Sabrina's guided reading lesson with a group of early readers. Notice that the students are working independently in literacy corners as the teachers collaborate within the natural context of the school day.

Figure 6.1 Linda and Sabrina confer after Sabrina's guided reading lesson.

Modeling and Coaching

The more experienced teacher models specific components for the less experienced teacher. This teacher provides coaching and guidance strategies to support the novice teacher as she begins to implement the literacy component in her own classroom. Andrea Fortner, a teacher at an elementary school in North Little Rock, Arkansas, describes this process. "When I first heard about writers' workshop, I had a million questions. I needed to see it implemented in a first-grade classroom. Julie is my mentor teacher; she observes and coaches me as I conduct mini-lessons and writing conferences with my students. I have learned so much from her; and my children's writing has improved because of what I've learned."

Clear and Relevant Language for Problem Solving

The teachers' interactions focus on problem-solving language around specific issues of teaching and learning. For instance, in the post-conference from a guided reading lesson, Laura prompts Paula to articulate her observations. "Tell me what you noticed," she says. As Paula discusses her notes, the two teachers engage in problem-solving language that is grounded in the children's processing behaviors.

How do you get there?

Adjustable and Self-Destructing Scaffolds

As the novice teacher acquires more competence in implementing a literacy component, the literacy coach (or mentor teacher) adjusts the scaffolding to accommodate this new level of understanding. For instance, when teachers first begin to implement guided reading groups in their literacy block, the coach scaffolds them with a guided reading observation form (Figure 6.2). In a preconference, they discuss the components of the guided reading lesson, and the teacher explains her rationale for selecting the particular book. As the teacher works with the children, the coach records observations on the form, which she uses in her follow-up conference with the teacher. At the conclusion of the conference, the coach leaves her notes with the teacher, who adds them to her reflective notebook. This observation guide serves a similar purpose to the checklists used by students to guide and assess their writing. With teachers, the guided reading observation form is a temporary scaffold that self-destructs when it is no longer needed.

Structured Routines

Teachers, like children, develop routines that guide and support their learning. When teachers develop a habit of collaborating around teaching and learning issues, this drives their professional development. Structured routines become an integral part of the school culture, including peer observations and follow-up con-

Figure 6.2 Guided reading observation form. (Appendix K provides a blank form.)

Guided Reading Observation Guide

Teacher Name __Angela__ Text Level __I__ Date __2-9-00__

Book Introduction	Comments
Holds book and discusses basic plot, characters, author, and illustrator.	Introduced meaning of folktale (Do you know what a folktale is)? Related this folktale to <u>Jack and the Beanstalk</u>. Discussed folktale characteristics and related those characteristics to the <u>Pot of Gold</u>. In this folktale, Grumble the Giant (the bad character) and the elf (the good character) know where it is! Let's look inside and see.
Actively involves students.	✔ (great!)
Emergent (A–B) Introduces the book and engages students in discussing pictures and story ideas. Repeats recurring language phrases and patterns, being careful to use the precise vocabulary of the story.	
Early (B–H) Introduces the book and engages students in meaningful discussions at the text level, allowing connections and oral predictions.	
Transitional (H–M) Introduces the book and engages students in linking text-to-text and text-to-life.	Engages students to predict story using pictures and previously established background knowledge. Used open-ended questions to encourage active discussions!
Emergent (A–B) Prompts to prediction of the first letter of an unknown word.	
Early (B–H) Prompts to first letter, word parts, or letter sequences.	
Transitional (H–M) Prompts to the visual analysis of a word as needed.	Grumble + Promise - Prompted to search for word parts and blend parts together. Related back to text.

First Reading	Comments
Provides the appropriate text for smooth orchestration of reading process.	
Student Reading	
Supplies each student with his or her own text.	
Provides the opportunity for each student to read independently at his or her own pace.	
Circulates among the group, observing each student's reading behavior.	
Prompts the student to initiate appropriate problem-solving strategies as needed.	What did you notice? Check it with your finger and think about what Grumble needs to do so he can find the tree.
After Reading	
Discusses the meaning of the story.	Open-ended discussion around characters and story ideas. Teacher prompted for deeper meaning of story.
Involves all the students.	
Prompts student to self-monitor by locating problem areas.	Did anyone mark a tricky part with their Post-it note (encouraging self-monitoring)? Responded to student who didn't understand—"and he may be still digging."
Adjusts language scaffolding to support strategy development.	
Teaches skills, as needed.	

ferences, coaching and mentoring sessions, and literacy team meetings that focus on student progress. For instance, when first-grade teacher Linda Wilsey is unsure about her teaching prompts during guided reading, she immediately schedules an observation and follow-up conference with Sabrina, a more experienced teacher. The teachers are supported by the principal, Mavis Cherry, who values peer collaboration as a necessary element of professional development. Here, it is important to note that the school has created a climate where collaborative problem solving is embedded in the routine structure of the teaching environment.

Assisted and Independent Work

It is critical that teachers have the opportunity to apply new learning to independent work. As a teacher becomes more competent on a particular literacy task, the role of the mentor teacher diminishes in that capacity. The movement from assisted to independent work is mediated by apprenticeship techniques of modeling, coaching, scaffolding, and fading. For example, at the beginning of the school year, Laura McKinney assists Paula Tiffany, the first-grade teacher, in organizing and implementing literacy corners into her classroom block. By the end of the year, Paula has developed expertise in this area, and she is recognized by colleagues across the state, who visit her classroom to observe her literacy corners in action. Here, Paula has become a mentor to other classroom teachers in two important ways: she collaborates with teachers in the organizational aspects of implementing literacy corners, and she demonstrates these details in a videotaped session that she shares with other teachers. The ultimate goal of learning is that teachers will become less dependent on outside assistance and more dependent on their internal resources and knowledge.

Transfer

Transfer of knowledge, skills, and strategies can be inferred when a teacher shows the ability to apply these understandings to different contexts and for different purposes. For instance, when teachers learn about processing behaviors in guided reading, their understanding of literacy corners begins to change. They use their knowledge of the reading process to select word-building activities that support guided reading levels. Also, they study children's writing development in relation to reading development. Here, teacher's knowledge moves from the procedural to the conceptual level, thus building the foundation for self-regulated learning.

The Arkansas Literacy Coaching Model

The Arkansas Literacy Coaching Model is grounded in our belief that true change occurs at the school level. For the past ten years, we've worked in elementary classrooms to support teachers in implementing changes in their assessment and literacy practices. The literacy model is documented in *Apprenticeship in Literacy* (Dorn, French, and Jones 1998) and the video staff development series *Organizing for Literacy* (Dorn 1999). Three years ago, we worked with Teresa Treat, a first-grade teacher in Conway, Arkansas, to pilot a literacy coaching model in a school setting. If you've viewed the video series *Organizing for Literacy*, you will recall a literacy curriculum that is based on apprenticeship theories at both the student and teacher levels. Teresa was the apprentice—new to this teaching approach—and Carla was her coach. In a similar way, I coached Carla as we applied our knowledge of learning theory to our work with Teresa. At the end of the school year, the first-grade students had achieved dramatic gains in their reading and writing levels. Based on these experiences, we acquired grant funds from the Arkansas Department of Education to implement an apprenticeship model—with literacy coaches and mentor teachers—in seven new schools with an average poverty level of 60 percent. At the end of the school year, the achievement gains for these first-grade students were evident on both performance assessments and a standardized test. Results from the writing assessment of 245 first-grade students revealed that 88 percent scored at advanced, proficient, or nearly proficient levels in all three areas—writing process, author's craft, and language conventions. In areas of text reading, we found similar results, with 85 percent of first graders reading at proficient or advanced reading levels. Furthermore, on a national standardized test, the overall reading score for most of the schools increased from twenty to fifty points over previous years. These results led to further expansion of the model to twenty-two new schools. What led to the accelerated change in these schools? We believe the specific design of this model was the key to the change process (Dorn and Williams 2000; Balkman 2001).

Design Features

A well-designed model is the basis for a high-quality implementation. At the same time, the model should be monitored and assessed periodically to determine how well it is working within a school culture. If the design is not working well, this provides a problem-solving context for examining specific issues within the model. For instance, in one school, the literacy coach noted that students' writing portfolios didn't show evidence of the revising and editing processes, so she scheduled an observation visit with the teacher. In the follow-up conference, the teacher revealed that she had changed writers' workshop schedule from daily sessions to two or three times weekly. Based on evidence from the students' writing folders in relation to writing standards, the coach guided the teacher to reflect on the role of writers' workshop in promoting her students' writing development. This problem-solving atmosphere resulted in a well-organized plan for supporting the teacher as she dealt with the challenges of scheduling this new component into her classroom structure. It is important to recognize that problems will arise when teachers implement a new literacy component; without support and feedback, the design might be adapted to accommodate the teacher's confusions and frustrations. When these adaptations occur, the affected areas (e.g., daily writers' workshop) can influence how well the students perform on related tasks (e.g., knowledge of the writing process).

This implies two distinct yet complementary design features: a high-quality model that represents a standard for accomplishing a specific goal, and a measure of accountability that links performance to instructional practices. Specifically, the design features of the Arkansas Literacy Coaching Model are as follows:

A Curriculum for Literacy This is the heartbeat of the model; thus reading and writing must take top priority in the classroom. The framework is designed to provide young learners with many opportunities to practice effective problem-solving strategies on increasingly more complex texts. In a curriculum for literacy, the classrooms devote three-and-a-half hours to reading, writing, and spelling literacy, including whole groups, small groups, and individual conferences.

High Standards A standard represents a goal for achieving proficiency on a specific task. Teachers use two important standards for assessing students' progress: the Arkansas State Standards, and the New Primary Literacy Standards in Reading and Writing (National Standards Primary Committee 1999). These standards provide teachers with a tool for studying a student's progress over time. How much new learning must the student acquire to reach the standard? Will the student need supplemental help from a reading specialist? How can the teacher provide classroom support (e.g., small groups, individual conferences) in the needed areas? These questions focus attention of the relationship of teaching to learning, while recognizing that some children will require supplemental support to achieve proficiency on a particular standard. Here, it is important to note that the standard is not low-

ered; rather, the intensity of the support is maximized to accommodate the needs of the student. In Chapter 2, we shared how reading and writing standards are linked to a classroom curriculum for literacy. Here, in Tables 6.1 and 6.2, the New Primary Literacy Standards are used as a conceptual framework for linking curriculum and assessment.

Model Classrooms That Become Learning Labs
Throughout this book, we have stressed the importance of good models for helping learners to visualize a goal of instruction. This theory took on new meaning for us as we talked with teachers about the challenges they experienced in implementing new approaches. Over and over again, we kept hearing the same com-

Table 6.1 The Connection Between Reading Standards, Classroom Components, and Classroom Assessments

Standard	Classroom Components	Classroom Assessments
1. Print-Sound Code		
Knowledge of letters and their sounds	Familiar reading	Observation survey
Reading words	Shared reading	Running records
	Guided reading	Teacher observation log
	Spelling workshop	Developmental spelling test
	Interactive writing	Conference notes
	Independent writing	Word study notebooks
	Literacy corners	Corner notebooks
	Writers' workshop	Student portfolios
2. Getting Meaning		
Accuracy	Familiar reading	Running records
Fluency	Independent reading	Teacher observation log
Self-monitoring and self-correcting	Shared reading	Conference notes
strategies	Guided reading	Reading checklists
Comprehension	Literature discussions	Comprehension guides
	Read-aloud	Written retellings
	Mini-lessons	Literature response logs
3. Reading Habit		
Independent and assisted reading	Familiar reading	Student interviews
Being read to	Independent reading	Teacher observation log
Discussing books	Read-aloud	Conference notes
Vocabulary	Literature discussions	Literature response logs
	Guided reading	Corner notebooks

Table 6.2 The Connection Between Writing Standards, Classroom Components, and Classroom Assessments

Standard	Classroom Components	Classroom Assessments
1. Writes Daily		
Writes daily	Interactive writing	Conference notes
Understands writing process	Journal writing	Writing checklists
	Writing-aloud	Student portfolios
	Writers' workshop	Writers' notebooks
	Mini-lessons	Writing rubrics
	Author's chair	Student publications
	Literacy corners	Corner notebooks
2. Purposes and Resulting Genres		
Narrative, informational, functional, responding to literature	Interactive writing	Conference notes
	Writing-aloud	Writing checklists
	Independent writing	Writing rubrics
	Writers' workshop	Student portfolios
	Mini-lessons	Writers' notebooks
	Author's chair	Student publications
	Literacy corners	Corner notebooks
	Literature discussions	Literature response logs
3. Language Use and Conventions		
Style and syntax	Interactive writing	Conference notes
	Writing-aloud	Writing checklists
	Independent writing	Writing rubrics
	Mini-lessons	Writing notebooks

ment: "I need to see how it looks." We know that without a model it is difficult to visualize the way a particular concept might look. Thus, literacy coaches work intensely with two or three teachers to implement the literacy framework in the classroom setting. These model classrooms become literacy learning labs where other teachers can observe the program in action. For instance, if the topic for a literacy team meeting is guided reading, prior to the meeting the classroom teachers are expected to schedule observation visits, take notes, and bring their comments to the literacy team meeting. This common experience provides the group with a shared context for discussing specific teaching and learning issues. The model classrooms are important elements of this design for two reasons: they provide a clear model of the program in action, and they allow time for reluctant teachers to observe the process before they are expected to implement it.

Coaching and Mentoring The ultimate goal of the model is to create systemic change within the school culture while building internal capacity for supporting the change process. This means that the true agents of change reside within the school doors—the teachers, the principal, and the support staff. In this model, the coaching and mentoring pieces are critical elements of the design. In year 1, the literacy coach works intensely with two or three first-grade teachers in implementing model classrooms. In year 2, the model classroom teachers become mentor teachers for other first-grade teachers, and the literacy coach works closely with second-grade teachers in implementing model classrooms. The process of coaching and mentoring continues into third grade. By the end of year 3, all classrooms resemble model classroom settings (see Figure 6.3). Along the way, the problem-solving atmosphere is cultivated by the coaching and mentoring elements of this design.

Accountability for Student Progress In our work with classroom teachers, we've developed specific benchmark behaviors that reflect a continuum of writing proficiency for kindergarten to third-grade writers. Furthermore,

many teachers have designed their school report cards to reflect these standards. For instance, Carla worked with Teresa Treat, a first-grade teacher, to construct an assessment card based on the development of a literacy processing system and aligned with the state and national standards. Appendix L gives two examples of report cards. Notice the relationship between the Example 1 report card and the literacy checklists from Chapter 3. Literacy coaches across the state have created similar types of report cards. At Sunnymede

Figure 6.3 Three-year design of literacy coaching model.

Year 1	**Year 2**	**Year 3**
Training of school-based literacy coach	University support for literacy coach	University support for literacy coach
Support from university coaches	↑ ↓ ↑	↑ ↓ ↑
↑ ↓ ↑	Intensive coaching for second-grade classroom teachers	Intensive coaching for third-grade classroom teachers
Intensive coaching for first-grade model classroom teachers	↑ ↓ ↑	↑ ↓ ↑
↑ ↓ ↑	Develops second-grade model classrooms	Implement third-grade model classrooms
Develops two first-grade model classrooms	Students from first-grade model classrooms move to these new model classrooms	Students from model classrooms move to these new model classrooms
↑ ↓ ↑	↑ ↓ ↑	↑ ↓ ↑
Other teachers schedule observation visits	Other second-grade teachers schedule observation visits	Other third-grade teachers schedule observation visits
↑ ↓ ↑	↑ ↓ ↑	↑ ↓ ↑
SLC scaffolds and supports other K–3 teachers—classroom demonstrations and literacy team meetings	Scaffolding and supports for other K–3 teachers—classroom demonstrations and literacy team meetings	Scaffold and support for other K–3 teachers—classroom demonstrations and literacy team meetings
	↓ ↓ ↑	↑ ↓ ↑
Building internal support	First-grade model classroom teachers mentor two new first-grade teachers	Second-grade model classroom teachers mentor new second-grade teachers
	↑ ↓ ↑	↑ ↓ ↑
	Kindergarten team is established with mentor teacher	K–1 teachers continue working together to support each other

Elementary in Fort Smith, Arkansas, Wyann Stanton, the literacy coach, and classroom teachers wrote a letter to parents (Example 2) that explained the school's grading system for reading levels.

Additionally, all literacy coaching schools use an assessment wall (Figure 6.4) to chart the students' progress in guided reading groups. The idea for the assessment wall was adapted from the work of David Kerbow and colleagues at the Center for School Improvement in Chicago (Kerbow, Gwynne, and Jacob 1999). We work closely with teachers to make the assessment wall a problem-solving tool for supporting children in their progression of reading development. We believe that all children should be making steady progress, with the possible exception of two groups: special education students (a very small group) and transfer students (those who have recently moved into the classroom). These two groups are coded with a colored dot on the front of the student's card. Additionally, letter codes for special services are recorded in the left-hand corner of the card, for instance, Reading Recovery, Early Literacy Groups, Booster Groups, Gifted and Talented, Occupational Therapy, and Speech. On the back of the card, the teachers record testing dates, text reading levels, and accuracy scores from running records. As children progress through guided reading levels, the teachers move their cards on the assessment wall.

Assessment Wall Description

The cards indicate on which reading level each group is within the classroom. Each color indicates the classroom; each card represents a student with a corresponding number on the front and the child's name on the back. The cards move as the students move within the reading groups. The moves are recorded on the front and back of the card with the date and appropriate level. Any special services received are recorded on the bottom of the card. The front and back are identical except for the student's name and formal testing on the back of the card.

The assessment wall coding system represents the special services each child receives. The services are documented on the front of the card.

RR	Reading Recovery
ELG	Early Literacy Group
BG	Booster Group (second grade)
GT	Gifted and Talented
OT/PT	Occupational/Physical Therapy
S	Speech
SE	Special Education
T	Transfer Student

The assessment wall makes the data visible, thus serving two important purposes: to study learning trends in student groups (e.g., Reading Recovery, special education, transfer students); and to study reading progression for all students in relation to proficiency standards. Later, we take a closer look at how the teachers at one high-poverty school use the assessment wall in their literacy team meetings.

Figure 6.4 Sunnymede Elementary's first-grade assessment wall.

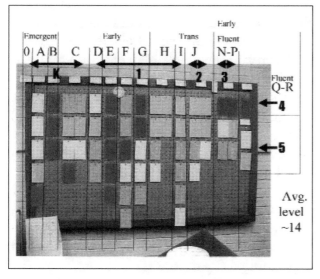

Supplementary Support for Students Because we have taught for most of our educational careers in high-poverty schools, we've experienced the link between poverty and limited opportunities. We've worked with excellent teachers who are passionate about the children they teach, and these are the same teachers who recognize that some children will need more intensive supplemental assistance to achieve their highest potential in reading. In literacy coaching schools, teachers are strong advocates of early intervention programs that provide the struggling reader with high-quality, intensive short-term help. Also, teachers realize the importance of monitoring students' progress during the primary grades and providing booster support, as needed, to coach students in specific literacy areas. During team meetings, the teachers use the assessment wall and student portfolios to study the reading progressions of children over time; they recognize the behaviors that indicate a student is lagging behind his or her peers; and they work together to provide a consistent approach for meeting the needs of the student.

Team Meetings That Focus on Teaching and Learning Issues Literacy team meetings provide a context for school-embedded professional development. In most schools, the entire primary staff (kindergarten to third grade) attends these weekly or bimonthly sessions. The literacy team meetings focus on teaching and learning issues, for example, administering and analyzing running records; planning constructive activities for literacy corners; designing minilessons for writers' workshop; studying writing portfolios for change over time in writing development; and analyzing videotaped lessons of various literacy components. In all schools, professional libraries are established to support teachers in their new learning, including video portfolios of lesson components from

model classrooms. The team meetings provide a context for supporting all the teachers toward achieving a common goal. For instance, at Green County Tech Elementary in Paragould, Arkansas, the kindergarten teachers worked together in implementing writers' workshop in their kindergarten program. As a result, by the end of the school year, the children had developed daily writing habits and acquired knowledge of early print conventions. This spillover effect was also evident in the writing programs of second-grade students. This implies that successful practices can create a ripple effect throughout a school, leading to changes in the literacy programs of kindergarten to third-grade teachers. The team meetings provide teachers with a supportive context for discussing how to implement these literacy components in their classroom structure.

Well-Articulated Plan to Monitor Progress It is critical that schools have a literacy map that includes both short- and long-term goals. In much the same way as we assess students' progress, schools need a set of benchmarks that enable them to monitor their own progress according to standard expectations. For instance, by November, we would expect literacy team meetings to be a routine part of the school climate. If this does not occur, then we can work with the school to identify the problem and develop a plan of action for dealing with it. In Fort Smith, Arkansas, the entire school district made the commitment to the Arkansas Comprehensive Literacy Model, including literacy coaches in all elementary schools. We collaborated with the district in developing a three-year literacy plan with benchmark indicators and time lines for implementation of specific components. This plan allows the district to monitor and assess its own progress against its own goals and expectations.

Technology A critical element of this design has been to create a climate that promotes active coaching and mentoring among teachers. The co-construction of knowledge implies that learners construct knowledge through problem-solving actions that are aimed toward accomplishing a common goal. Can we create a problem-solving network for teachers who are located across wide geographical regions in Arkansas? To answer this question, we use a listserv for each group: model classroom teachers and literacy coaches. We, along with Mike Moss and Stephanie Copes (two university coaches), occasionally join the listserv discussions and provide specialized support in particular areas. However, the intention of the listserv is to put the teachers in contact with each other, thus developing a collaborative network for supporting their professional development. For instance, Laura McKinney developed a series of spelling lessons and sent them as e-mail attachments to the literacy coaches, who provided feedback. The guided reading observation form (Figure 6.2) was refined over the listserv, after many coaches and classroom teachers had used it in their own school settings. From time to time, specific requests are given over the listserv, for instance, compiling a set of good read-aloud books and ways to use these texts with students. At the end of the school year, Linda and Mike examined the productivity of the listserv as a technological tool for guiding active problem solving among teachers and coaches. We discovered that the teachers had written nearly one thousand e-mails to each other during a one-year period. Furthermore, when we studied the types of e-mail correspondences, it became evident that the teachers and coaches had indeed used technology as a tool for co-constructing knowledge. Distinctive categories began to emerge, for instance, planning for team meetings; using the assessment wall; implementing literacy corners; spelling workshop; struggling readers; writers' workshop; book introductions; grouping for guided reading; ESL students; reporting data; and teaching spelling. The amazing point about this process was that in most cases the first e-mail seemed to initiate a chain of problem-solving responses. In other words, the teachers and coaches resolved the problems on their own, with little or no intervention from us. This represents a critical aspect of self-regulated learning.

In this section, we've discussed the design of the Arkansas Literacy Coaching Model. Now, we share a typical school day in the schedule of a literacy coach. First, we look at Donnie's schedule in year 1 of the model; then we briefly look at changes that occur in year 2, as Donnie moves into second grade and the first-grade model teachers become mentor teachers for their peers.

A Literacy Coach Schedule: Donnie Skinner, Boone Park Elementary

Donnie Skinner is a literacy coach at Boone Park Elementary School, a high-poverty school (97 percent) in the North Little Rock School District. During the implementation year, Donnie provides intensive coaching to two first-grade teachers, Sabrina Kessler and Julie Dibee. Donnie's major responsibilities are to work with Julie and Sabrina in creating model first-grade classrooms that can serve as learning labs for the primary division. Thus, she alternates her mornings between the two first-grade classrooms. At the beginning of the year, Donnie and the two teachers worked together to set up guided reading groups and assisted writing groups, and to implement the organizational format for the literacy curriculum. Donnie has guided the teachers to establish the classroom structure, although she realizes that all components will not be working smoothly until later in the school year. The important point is that the teachers and students will develop routines for the literacy schedule, then refine these components within the structure of the established format. For instance, although the teachers include the spelling block in their morning schedule, Donnie doesn't expect them to fully implement this component until later in the school year. She understands this is a learning process for the teachers, as for herself, and each day she reflects on their progress as it relates to their past and future goals.

On this morning, as always, Donnie begins by preparing for the day ahead. As she looks over her schedule (see Appendix M), she realizes the importance of managing her time in a productive way so as to accomplish the multiple roles of her job. Donnie never loses sight of her goal, that is, to create a school climate that leads to self-regulated teachers. She smiles as she thinks about how well Sabrina and Julie are doing in their classrooms, and she knows that they will be strong mentor teachers for Linda and Andrea during the following year.

As the clock approaches 8:00, Donnie is on her way to Sabrina's classroom to observe the students during the independent reading block. Here she can observe children and take a few running records on selected students. Donnie feels this is important for her professional development; also, it enables her to capture snapshots of the students' reading behaviors. She spends about twenty minutes in Sabrina's classroom. Sabrina doesn't look up as Donnie walks into the room, for she is absorbed in listening to a student who is reading a familiar text. Donnie sits beside Michael as he reads a level H text—she recalls that Sabrina has just moved him to a new guided reading group earlier this week. Across the room, Sabrina and Donnie exchange glances, a little smile that indicates Michael is doing fine at this reading level. Later in the day, they will

find the time to share their observations of the children, but right now the focus is on observing the students as they independently read books from their familiar reading baskets.

During the next twenty-minute block, Donnie observes Sabrina as she engages the students in a shared reading experience. The students read two familiar poems, and Sabrina coaches them to locate rhyming words and classify them according to sound and letter patterns. Sabrina reminds the students that she will place these poems in the rhythm and rhyme corner for further practice. This whole-group lesson serves as a natural springboard for the spelling block. Donnie notes Sabrina's teaching is focused and explicit, and the students are responsive to the instruction.

The first-grade spelling lessons are coming along well: Sabrina is using spelling words to help the children acquire strategies for learning about words (see Chapter 4). Today, Donnie plans to observe Sabrina as she introduces words for teaching strategies of analogy. As she watches the lesson, she records notes that she will share with Sabrina. Later, when Donnie confers with Sabrina, she provides her with learning opportunities at two levels: learning about the spelling lesson, and learning how to conduct a conference. This is on-the-job training—true apprenticeship learning—for Donnie knows that Sabrina is acquiring experiences that will influence her own mentoring interactions with new teachers next year.

After the spelling lesson, Sabrina instructs the children to check the task board for literacy corner assignments. She calls the first guided reading group, and Donnie prepares to observe. Yesterday, Sabrina had talked with Donnie about the reading strategies of the group and her rationale for selecting this particular book. Here, Sabrina shares her concerns with Donnie and recruits her help: "I'm concerned that I might not be asking the right questions to promote the orchestration process. The children should be reading with more smoothness and expression. Can you observe me to see if my prompting might be interfering with their fluency?" With this goal in mind, Donnie observes the lesson. Afterward she coaches Sabrina to reflect on her teaching. She begins with the prompt, "How do you think the lesson went?" As the teachers discuss specific examples, Donnie leads from behind, while encouraging Sabrina to self-assess her own teaching in relation to her own goals. At the end of the conference, Donnie makes a copy of her notes, which she leaves with Sabrina to include in her reflection log.

Donnie returns to her office to reflect on the day thus far. She uses this brief period of time to organize her thoughts, summarize her observations, and record these notations in her reflection log. She makes a few notations to talk with Sabrina about a reading group that appears ready to use a word study notebook at the spelling corner. This is a new component for Sabrina, and Donnie will need to demonstrate this approach with a small group of students. As Donnie flips through the last few pages, she notes that her coaching role is beginning to shift as Sabrina is becoming more independent and self-assured with all literacy components. She glances at her watch, realizes it is already lunchtime, and heads toward the lounge to join the first-grade teachers for lunch.

After lunch, Donnie returns to her office to prepare for the literacy team meeting, to be held that afternoon. The meetings occur once a week, and lately she has been working with the teachers on mini-lessons in writing. She notes that the mini-lessons tend to last too long. Her goal is to encourage teachers to reflect on the importance of clear and memorable examples for teaching a process. Recently, several of the coaches have shared videotaped lessons, and this afternoon Donnie plans to use them—one

from Laura McKinney's school and another from Angela Owen's—to guide the teachers to identify key principles that support productive mini-lessons. Quickly, she makes a few notes, for example, short and focused lessons, clear examples, explicit language, and application to practice. Donnie glances at her watch and notices that she has just enough time to check the listserv. This morning, she had sent a message to the literacy coaches regarding a student in Julie's room, whom she is worried about because he has just transferred into the school; his reading level is much lower than the other students'. Although there are no messages, Donnie expects to have responses from the coaches by the end of the day.

It is nearly 11:50, and Donnie is eager to work with her own students. She spends forty minutes each day teaching a small group of children. This is for her own professional development. During the last three weeks, she has been teaching a group of five students who are reading trade books. "It is different," Donnie says, "working with the higher reading levels. Most of my past teaching experience has been with emergent and early groups, and I really need to spend time with transitional and fluent readers." The time goes quickly, and Donnie leaves the children with a promise to return tomorrow.

At 12:30, Donnie heads to Sabrina's classroom for writers' workshop. Donnie and Sabrina enjoy writers' workshop. In fact, Sabrina comments, "It's my favorite part of the day. I just have to watch myself to be sure that I don't spend too long on mini-lessons and conferences." "Yes," Donnie agrees. "That's the hard part, and I have to keep reminding myself of the purpose behind everything I do with the children. That helps to keep me focused." Then she asks Sabrina, "Would you like for me to watch as you conference with your children?" Sabrina accepts Donnie's offer with enthusiasm. Donnie observes as she confers with four students, and during the last ten minutes of writers' workshop, Donnie and Sabrina confer together while the students continue to write independently. Here, Donnie coaches Sabrina to reflect on her own teaching, as related to the specific areas that she had identified earlier. As always, Donnie makes a copy of her notes and leaves them with Sabrina to include in her reflection log.

During the next seventy-five minutes, Donnie visits several classrooms, demonstrating various literacy components and coaching teachers in these areas. This is a critical part of the literacy design, and Donnie plans her schedule carefully to accommodate the teachers. First, she heads to a kindergarten classroom where she models an interactive writing lesson. The kindergarten teachers are very interested in the writing component and several times lately, Donnie has scheduled demonstration lessons in these classrooms. She knows how helpful it can be for teachers to simply observe and record notes. The lesson lasts about fifteen minutes, and as the children are writing in their journals, Donnie and the teacher quietly discuss the lesson. As Donnie prepares to leave, the teacher asks, "Would you come back next week and watch me teach an interactive writing lesson?" Donnie and the teacher schedule a time, and Donnie moves to a second-grade classroom where she demonstrates a mini-lesson on sticking to a topic, then conducts two writing conferences with second-grade students. The second-grade teacher is an observer, recording notes and questions for Donnie when they confer at a later time. Thirty minutes later, Donnie is on her way to Andrea's first-grade classroom to observe her teaching a science lesson on planets. The students are using a Venn diagram to compare the planets Earth and Mars. Later that afternoon, Andrea and Donnie will use this information to create a set of literacy task cards for the science corner.

The next part of the day is an important one: the time to reflect and document the day's learning. It has been a full day, and Donnie realizes that she will need to capture the key learning experiences and observations. She searches her calendar for a time to meet with the four kindergarten teachers to discuss writers' workshop. She jots herself a note to arrange lunch together this week; also, she remembers a great videotaped lesson from Cathy Worley's kindergarten classroom in Camden-Fairview, and she makes a note to share this tape during lunch. Then she recalls that the kindergarten teachers at Green County Tech are implementing writers' workshop in their classrooms. In fact, at the last meeting with literacy coaches, Kim Mitchell had shared the writing portfolios of several kindergarten students in her school. Donnie makes a notation to send Kim an e-mail about this. As Donnie continues to record her thoughts, she remembers her concern about the student who had just transferred into the school. She gathers her materials and walks down the hallway to see Robin Whitten, the Reading Recovery and early literacy teacher. Robin is just completing her lesson with a small group of second graders. Donnie and Robin discuss the new student, who needs Reading Recovery services. "Yes," Robin says, "I've already tested him, and I plan to pick him up as soon as my next student discontinues. But, for now, I can teach him during my flex-time each morning." When Donnie returns to her office, she continues to reflect on the day. As she opens her e-mail, she smiles when she reads the six responses to her earlier message. As always, the coaches offer good advice, the first response being that of supplemental assistance from the Reading Recovery teacher. She glances at her watch and walks to the literacy team meeting.

The classroom teachers are already moving the cards on the assessment wall (Figure 6.5). The results look good; in fact, Donnie notices that only two cards on the entire wall have red dots, which stand for special education children. The reduction in special referrals at the school has been amazing. When one of the teachers comments on this fact, Sabrina remarks, "It's because we know more about how children are learning, and we're working together to help them before they get so far behind." "Yes," Julie says. "Too many kids were being referred who just had confusions." A teacher expresses concern about students who are not at proficiency level on the assessment wall, and Robin offers to provide the students with supplemental support in a small-group early literacy program. The team meeting lasts one hour, with the primary focus on mini-lessons in writers' workshop. Even after the meeting ends, many of the teachers linger behind, continuing to discuss teaching and learning issues. It has been a full and productive day.

By the end of the implementation year, Donnie knows that Sabrina and Julie are well prepared to become mentor teachers for the other first-grade teachers. Now she focuses on sustained coaching in the second-grade classrooms. (See Appendix M for her schedule and Figure 6.6 for a second-grade teacher's sched-

ule.) As she did last year, she continues to support other teachers with demonstration lessons and class visits. However, over the next two years, her major responsibility is to work closely with the second- and third-grade teachers in creating model classrooms. These teachers are not new to the literacy approach because they were active participants in team meetings and classroom visits during the previous year.

Donnie and the model classroom teachers share a dialogue journal. In these daily entries, Donnie and the teacher problem-solve about teaching components and student learning. Donnie believes the dialogue journal is another way of scaffolding teachers and promoting a collaborative environment.

Figure 6.5 Boone Park teachers moving reading group cards on assessment wall.

Dialogue Journal Excerpt

Donnie,
Thanks for the suggestion. It really helped! Those reading workshop ideas were also of great assistance. You know, sometimes I really worry that I might mess up, or not get through to the kids, but I know mistakes will be made, and I won't get everything right the first time around. I just thank heavens for tomorrows and second chances. You are helping me to become a better teacher and an effective planner! Thank you.
Chan
P.S. Exactly how do we choose spelling words? Is it the skill we want to teach or words with similarities? I don't know if I am comfortable or even if I fully understand the selection process.

Chantele,
Good question about spelling. We try to pick out words related to reading and writing. It is a combination of skills and strategies. I tried to think of words that can be sorted into categories but also words that teach the skill like the compound word we had. They will be doing spelling and word sorting activities in their word building/spelling corner so I am trying to prepare them by modeling sorts. We can pick spelling

Figure 6.6 Second- and Third-Grade Literacy Schedules

8:00–8:20	***Independent Reading:*** Students read independently as teacher circulates around the room, observing and conferencing. Teacher keeps observation log and records notes on students, including running records and comprehension checks.
8:20–8:40	***Strategy-Based Mini-Lesson:*** Whole-group mini-lessons focus on comprehension strategies. Teacher uses clear demonstrations and explicit teaching.
8:40–9:55	***Small-Group Reading:*** Students attend guided reading groups that are aimed toward their instructional zones. Also, students participate in literature discussion groups based on needs and interest levels. (During this block of time, other students are working in literacy corners [word study, math, science, language arts] or on reading/writing projects.)
9:55–10:15	***Spelling/Word Study:*** Whole-group lessons focus on word study skills. Resources, such as dictionaries, thesauruses, and word study notebooks, are used to analyze words and explore meanings.
10:15–11:15	***Writers' Workshop:*** Whole-group mini-lessons focus on areas of organization, processes, skills, strategies, and craft (10 minutes). Students write independently and teacher conducts five to seven teacher-scheduled conferences and one to two student-scheduled conferences each day. Peer conferences and small-group conferences are held as needed. (See sign-up schedule on wall.) Published work is shared in author's chair.
11:15–12:00	***Lunch/Recess***
12:00–12:30	***Special Activities (Computer, P.E., Library, Music)***
12:30–12:45	***Read-Aloud:*** Teacher reads aloud to students. The read-aloud can be related to mini-lessons in reading/writing or to content-area studies.
12:45–1:45	***Math:*** Whole-group lessons focus on clear demonstrations and explicit teaching. Students practice computation and problem-solving strategies in independent and group work. Teacher works with groups of students who need extra help. Students work together to solve problems, discuss strategies, and record solutions in their math logs. (These are carried over to the literacy corners.)
1:45–2:00	***Recess***
2:00–2:45	***Content-Area Study:*** Students engage in a variety of social studies and science activities. These activities are carried over to the literacy corners (in the morning block), including experiments, recording information in science logs, conducting research, and reading content-area books.
2:45–3:00	***Closure:*** Teacher guides students to reflect on the day's learning and to share with each other. Students can write in journals or work on homework during this time.
3:00–3:20	***Car riders dismissed at 3:00. Bus riders dismissed at 3:10 to 3:15.***
3:30–4:30	***Literacy Team Meetings on Tuesday Each Week:*** Bring student writing folders. Plan to change guided reading groups on assessment wall.

words out together soon so we can think aloud while we do it. I think it will help.

Yes, I thank every day for tomorrows! My whole life is a trial and error! Hopefully, I can bring what I learned last year to help us this year and also gain more insight in the process. I certainly have. You are so positive.

Thanks,
Donnie

The risk-taking atmosphere is evident in Donnie's comments to Chantele, a second-grade teacher: "I thank every day for tomorrows! My whole life is a trial and error! Hopefully, I can bring what I learned last year to help us this year and also gain more insight in the process." As teachers work together, they must trust each other and be willing to share their frustrations and concerns as they implement new changes in their teaching practices.

Closing Thoughts

In this chapter, we have shared an apprenticeship approach for coaching and scaffolding teachers. The teachers in this chapter are learners who continue to extend their professional development each day through peer collaboration. The same principles that we apply to children are applied to teachers. Throughout this book, we have shared with you the stories of teachers and children learning together in real-life situations. We have emphasized the social and cognitive sides to learning. In closing, we leave you with one last thought. The goal of teaching is to create conditions where learners have the knowledge and motivation to extend their own learning to higher and higher levels.

Appendixes

Appendix A

Emergent Reading Behaviors: Attending to Print

Student _____ **Date** _____

Book Title/Text Level _____

Reading Behavior	Observed Behavior	Not Observed	Comments
Attends to print using known words.			
Points to words with 1-1 matching on 1 and 2 lines of text.			
Fluently reads some high-frequency words.			
Articulates first letter in unknown words.			
Notices unknown words and searches for cues in picture and print.			
Uses a special key word from ABC chart or letter book to help with solving words.			
Rereads to cross-check first letter with meaning and structure cues.			

Appendix B

Emergent Writing Behaviors: Encoding and Writing Fluency

Student _____ **Date** _____

Written Text _____

Writing Behavior	Observed Behavior	Not Observed	Comments
Writes known letters with correct formation.			
Uses spaces between words with greater accuracy.			
Recognizes link between known sounds and related letters; slowly articulates word with blended sounds.			
Uses ABC chart or letter book as resource for sound-letter links.			
Writes a few high-frequency words with accuracy; begins to acquire a writing vocabulary that reflects attention to reading.			
Uses first part of known words to help write parts of unknown words.			
Includes new words from reading experiences in writing.			

Appendix C

Comprehension Guide for Story Retelling

Student _____ Date _____

Story _____ Text Level _____

Comprehension Guide	Unprompted Behavior	Prompted Behavior	Comments
Retells story in logical and sequential order.			
Discusses the main and secondary characters in the story.			
Describes the setting of the story.			
Uses language phrases, book talk, and/or special vocabulary from the story.			
Detects the problem and solution in the story.			
Includes supporting details from the story.			
Connects story to other texts (text-to-text).			
Responds to story at a personal level (text-to-life).			
Describes the story ending.			

Shaping Literate Minds: Developing Self-Regulated Learners by Linda J. Dorn and Carla Soffos. Copyright © 2001. Stenhouse Publishers

Appendix D

Early Reading Behaviors: Decoding Strategies

Student _____ **Date** _____

Book Title/Text Level _____

Reading Behavior	Observed Behavior	Not Observed	Comments
Self-monitors reading with greater ease; uses known words and patterns to check on reading.			
Searches through words in a left-to-right sequence; blends letters into sounds; repeats word as if to confirm.			
Takes words apart at the larger unit of analysis.			
Reads high-frequency words fast, fluently, and automatically.			
Becomes faster at noticing errors and initiates multiple attempts to self-correct.			

Appendix E

Early Writing Behaviors: Encoding and Writing Fluency

Student _____ **Date** _____

Written Text _____

Writing Behavior	Observed Behavior	Not Observed	Comments
Begins to notice common misspellings; circles words that do not look right; uses a simple dictionary to self-correct; uses resources to self-check work; acquires a writing vocabulary that reflects reading.			
Analyzes sequence of sounds and records corresponding letters; segments and blends sounds in words with greater ease.			
Constructs words using larger units of sound-to-letter patterns; becomes faster and more efficient at writing words.			
Applies knowledge of onset and rime patterns for writing unknown words.			
Notices similarities between word patterns.			

Appendix F

Writing Checklist for Narrative Writing (Purposes and Craft)

Student _____ Date _____

Text _____

Writing Behavior	Observed Behavior	Not Observed	Comments
Uses an interesting introduction that grabs the attention of the reader.			
Writes events and ideas in logical and sequential order that makes sense to the reader.			
Sustains the idea throughout the piece.			
Uses dialogue.			
Uses strong vocabulary and good word choices.			
Uses individual voice.			
Uses reaction phrases.			
Uses transition and time cue words to support flow.			
Ties story together with creative or imaginative ending.			

Appendix G

Transitional Reading Behaviors: Decoding Strategies

Student _____ **Date** _____

Book Title/Text Level _____

Reading Behavior	Observed Behavior	Not Observed	Comments
Expands reading vocabulary; shows interest in unfamiliar words that she reads.			
Solves multisyllabic words by noticing parts within the words.			
Quickly takes words apart at the larger unit of analysis.			
Uses word meanings to solve word problems (prefixes, suffixes, roots, compound parts).			
Reads longer texts with greater accuracy and fluency. Preprocesses error before mistake is made.			

Shaping Literate Minds: Developing Self-Regulated Learners by Linda J. Dorn and Carla Soffos. Copyright © 2001. Stenhouse Publishers

Appendix H

Transitional Writing Behaviors

Student _____ **Date** _____

Written Text _____

Writing Behavior	Observed Behavior	Not Observed	Comments
Expands writing vocabulary; includes new and unusual words.			
Attends to syllables when writing words; problem-solves with greater ease and fluency.			
Writes increasingly longer texts with greater accuracy and speed.			
Shows flexibility with word choice; tries out different ways of saying a message with the same meaning; revises word choices in writing process; uses a thesaurus as a resource.			
Uses dictionaries, editing checklists, and other resources to self-correct writing.			

Appendix I

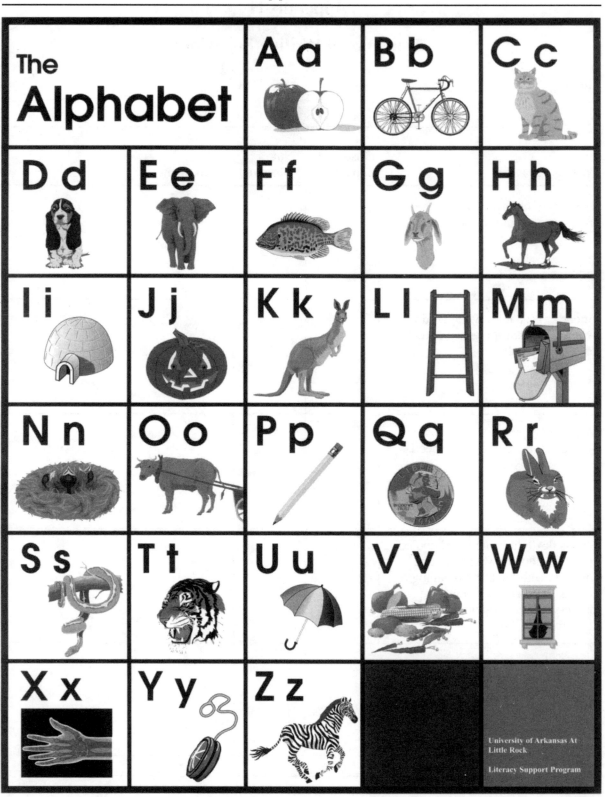

The Alphabet

A a

B b

C c

D d

E e

F f

G g

H h

I i

J j

K k

L l

M m

N n

O o

P p

Q q

R r

S s

T t

U u

V v

W w

X x

Y y

Z z

University of Arkansas At Little Rock

Literacy Support Program

Appendix J

Name Task Examples by Literacy Level

1. **Syllables (Emergent)**
   - Choose a name.
   - Clap the name.
   - Put the name together by syllables.
   - Write the name.

2. **Syllables (Emergent)**
   - Line up the names and category cards.
   - Choose a name.
   - Clap the name.
   - Sort the names under the correct category card.
   - Write the name.

3. **Building names (Emergent)**
   - Choose a friend's name.
   - Make the name with magnetic letters.
   - Draw a circle, and sort the letters by features.
   - Write the sorted letters.

4. **Building names (Emergent)**
   - Choose a friend's name.
   - Make the name with magnetic letters.
   - Write the name.

5. **Matching picture to name (Emergent)**
   - Line up the pictures and names.
   - Choose a name.
   - Match the name with the picture.
   - Write the name.

6. **Sorting names by categories (Emergent)**
   - Line up the category cards (number that represents letters in name).
   - Choose a name.
   - Count the number of letters in the name.
   - Sort the name under the correct category card.
   - Write the sorted name.

7. **Sorting by "boy" and "girl" categories (Emergent)**
   - Line up the names and category cards.
   - Choose a name.
   - Sort the name under the correct category card.
   - Write the sorted names.

8. **Sorting names by using the ABC chart (Emergent)**
   - Line up the names and category cards.
   - Choose a name.
   - Sort the name under the correct beginning sound from the ABC chart.
   - Write the sorted names, and highlight the beginning sounds.

9. **ABC order using first name (Early)**
   - Line up the names.
   - Put the names in ACB order by using first letter.
   - Write the names in ABC order.

10. **Matching the first and last names to the picture (Early)**
    - Line up the names.
    - Match the first name to the last name.
    - Match the name to the picture.
    - Write the first and last names.

11. **Identifying consonants (Early)**
    - Line up the names.
    - Choose a name.
    - Write the name.
    - Highlight the consonant letters in the name.

12. **Identifying beginning consonant digraphs in names (Early)**
    - Line up the names.
    - Read the names.
    - Write the names, and highlight the beginning digraph.

13. **Sorting names by endings (Early)**
    - Line up the names and the letter tiles.
    - Choose a name.
    - Sort the name under the letter tile that stands for the sound you hear at the end of the name.
    - Write the name, and highlight the letter that stands for the ending sound.

14. **Identifying vowels (Early)**
    - Line up the names.
    - Choose a name.
    - Write the name.
    - Highlight the vowels in the name.

15. **Sorting names by using ending (*Y,* silent *e, r* controlled vowels, *a* at the end) (Early)**
    - Line up the names and category cards.
    - Choose a name.
    - Sort the name under the correct category card that stands for the sound you hear at the end of the name.
    - Write the name, and highlight the letter that stands for the ending sound.

Shaping Literate Minds: Developing Self-Regulated Learners by Linda J. Dorn and Carla Soffos. Copyright © 2001. Stenhouse Publishers

16. Sorting names that have double consonants in the middle (Early)
- Line up the names.
- Clap the name.
- Write the name, and draw a line between the double consonant.

17. Sorting names by vowel digraphs (Early)
- Line up the names and category cards (*ay, ai*).
- Choose a name.
- Sort the names under the correct category card.
- Write the sorted names, and highlight the vowel digraph in each name.

18. ABC order using first and second letters (Early)
- Line up the name cards.
- Put the names in ABC order.
- Write the sorted names.

19. Syllables (separation of syllables by line) (Early-Transitional)
- Line up the names.
- Choose a name.
- Clap the name.
- Write the name, and draw lines to separate the name into syllables.

Appendix K

Guided Reading Observation Guide

Teacher Name _____ Text Level _____ Date _____

Book Introduction	**Comments**
Holds book and discusses basic plot, characters, author, and illustrator.	
Actively involves students.	
Emergent (A–B) Introduces the book and engages students in discussing pictures and story ideas. Repeats recurring language phrases and patterns, being careful to use the precise vocabulary of the story.	
Early (B–H) Introduces the book and engages students in meaningful discussions at the text level, allowing connections and oral predictions.	
Transitional (H–M) Introduces the book and engages students in linking text-to-text and text-to-life.	
Emergent (A–B) Prompts to prediction of the first letter of an unknown word.	
Early (B–H) Prompts to first letter, word parts, or letter sequences.	
Transitional (H–M) Prompts to the visual analysis of a word as needed.	

Shaping Literate Minds: Developing Self-Regulated Learners by Linda J. Dorn and Carla Soffos. Copyright © 2001. Stenhouse Publishers

	Comments
First Reading	
Provides the appropriate text for smooth orchestration of reading process.	
Student Reading	
Supplies each student with his or her own text.	
Provides the opportunity for each student to read independently at his or her own pace.	
Circulates among the group, observing each student's reading behavior.	
Prompts the student to initiate appropriate problem-solving strategies as needed.	
After Reading	
Discusses the meaning of the story.	
Involves all the students.	
Prompts student to self-monitor by locating problem areas.	
Adjusts language scaffolding to support strategy development.	
Teaches skills, as needed.	

Appendix L

Report Cards (Example 1)

Evaluation Codes

4	Advanced (95–100%)	Consistently works above grade level.
3	Proficient (80–94%)	Consistently meets grade-level expectations.
2	Basic (70–79%)	Work is nearing grade level but still working below expectations.
1	Below basic (64% or below)	Work is consistently below grade level.

Spelling	1	2	3	4
Learns assigned words.				
Spells learned words correctly in daily work.				

Reading				
Expected reading levels				
Current reading level				

Comprehension				
Understands role of author and illustrator.				
Uses prior knowledge to make predictions, draw conclusions.				
Retells story in logical, sequential order.				
Discusses characters, setting.				
Detects problem, solution.				
Recalls important details.				
Responds to story; text-to-text/text-to-life.				

Decoding Strategies/Reading Fluency 1st Nine Weeks				
One-to-one, directionality, return sweep.				
Reads small core of sight words fluently in easy texts.				
Notices unknown words in print.				
Rereads/searches for meaning, structure, visual cues in text.				
Articulates first letter in unknown words.				
Reads patterned text, using memory for story structure.				

Decoding Strategies/Reading Fluency 2d Nine Weeks				
Reads a core of sight words fluently.				
Faster at noticing errors (meaning, structure, visual errors).				
Initiates multiple attempts to self-correct.				
Rereads/searches for meaning, structure, and visual cues in text.				
Searches through unknown words in a left-right sequence; begins to attend to blends, ending, digraphs, and vowel patterns.				

Shaping Literate Minds: Developing Self-Regulated Learners by Linda J. Dorn and Carla Soffos. Copyright © 2001. Stenhouse Publishers

Decoding Strategies/Reading Fluency 3d Nine Weeks

Reads a large core of sight words fluently.				
Notices mismatch in meaning, structure, or visual cues with ease.				
Rereads/searches for meaning, structure, and visual cues with ease.				
Initiates multiple attempts to self-correct.				
Searches through unknown words attending to larger units; blends digraphs, vowel patterns, onset and rime patterns with ease.				

Decoding Strategies/Reading Fluency 4th Nine Weeks

Reads a larger core of sight words fluently (about 100).				
Reads longer text accurately and fluently.				
Notices mismatch in meaning, structure, and visual cues with greater ease.				
Searches through unknown words attending to larger units; blends digraphs, vowel patterns, onset and rime patterns with greater ease.				
Self-corrects reading on the run.				

Handwriting

Forms letters correctly.				
Uses lines correctly.				
Uses proper spacing.				
Writes neatly and legibly.				
Reversals and confusions.				

Writing

Encoding/Writing Fluency 1st Nine Weeks

Generates topics for writing.				
Hears/records sounds in words (beginning, ending, some vowel sounds).				
Uses known letters, words, ABC chart as resources for sound/letter links.				
Rereads to clarify message by adding or deleting information.				
Demonstrates some awareness of punctuation and capitalization.				

Encoding/Writing Fluency 2d Nine Weeks

Generates topics for writing.				
Writes for different purposes (lists, letters, invitations, reports) with limited understanding.				
Hears/records sounds in words with ease.				
Writes in logical, sequential order using transition words to support flow.				
Rereads to clarify message by adding or deleting information.				
Identifies/self-corrects some punctuation, capitalization, and spelling.				

Writing Purposes/Craft 3d Nine Weeks				
Generates topics for writing.				
Writes for different purposes (lists, letters, invitations, reports) with more understanding.				
Writing may include opening phrase or sentence ("Yesterday," "How does a butterfly become a butterfly?").				
Writing is in logical, sequential order using transition words as needed.				
Writing includes supporting ideas.				
Writing may include good word choice (strong verbs, adjectives, adverbs), voice, reaction phrases, or dialogue.				
Writing may include a sense of closure ("The end"; "Now it is a butterfly").				
Rereads to clarify message by adding or deleting information.				
Identifies/self-corrects some punctuation, capitalization, and spelling.				
Writing Purposes/Craft 4th Nine Weeks				
Generates topics for writing.				
Writes for different purposes (lists, letters, invitations, reports) with greater understanding.				
Writing may include opening phrase or sentence ("One day," "Do you know about the moon?").				
Writing is in logical, sequential order (beginning, middle, end).				
Writing includes some good word choice (strong verbs, adjectives, adverbs), voice, reaction phrases, or dialogue.				
Writing includes a sense of closure ("It was a great day!"; "I hope you enjoyed learning about the moon").				
Rereads to clarify message by adding or deleting information.				
Identifies/self-corrects more punctuation, capitalization, and spelling.				

Shaping Literate Minds: Developing Self-Regulated Learners by Linda J. Dorn and Carla Soffos. Copyright © 2001. Stenhouse Publishers

Report Cards (Example 2)

This letter to parents accompanies the Sunnymede Elementary first-grade report card.

Dear First-Grade Parents,

We hope this helps you understand your child's reading grade on the First-Grade report card. Learning to read is the most important goal for your child in the First Grade. Your child's teacher will write on the report card which *classroom reading level* (not grade level) your child is on, and which *classroom reading level* (not grade level) your child *should* be on. This is so you will know if your child needs your help to catch up.

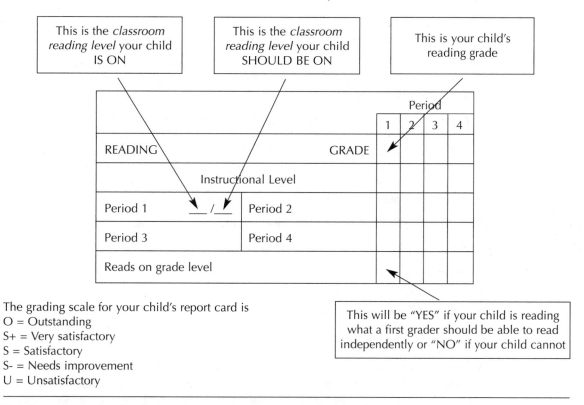

The grading scale for your child's report card is
O = Outstanding
S+ = Very satisfactory
S = Satisfactory
S- = Needs improvement
U = Unsatisfactory

The classroom reading levels that appear in the Sunnymede Elementary report card are based on the following expectations for first grade:

End of 1st Nine Weeks
A = Reading on or above level 4
P = Reading on level 3
B = Reading below level 3
BB = Not participating in reading learning

End of 3d Nine Weeks
A = Reading on or above level 14
P = Reading on level 13
B = Reading below level 13
BB = Not participating in reading learning

End of 2d Nine Weeks
A = Reading on or above level 8
P = Reading on level 7
B = Reading below level 7
BB = Not participating in reading learning

End of 4th Nine Weeks
A = Reading on or above level 17
P = Reading on level 16
B = Reading below level 16
BB = Not participating in reading learning

A = Advanced; P = Proficient; B = Basic; BB = Below Basic.

Appendix M

Literacy Coach Schedule for First Year

This schedule is organized to provide sustained coaching in two first-grade classrooms with the goal of developing first-grade model learning labs. The coach will support each model teacher during the entire literacy block at least two days each week for a full year. The following year, these model teachers will become mentor teachers for other first-grade teachers. In the afternoon, the coach will work with K–3 teachers each day for one hour and will teach a small group of students for thirty minutes daily.

7:45–8:00   ***Preparation:*** Gather materials to coach in one first-grade model classroom, then repeat the same schedule the next day in the other model classroom.

8:00–8:20   ***Independent Reading:*** Observe model teacher and students during independent reading. Take at least one running record of a student's reading. Record notes for sharing with the teacher during a later conference.

8:20–10:45   ***Sustained Coaching in Model Classroom:*** Use the coaching design to support the first-grade teacher in implementing all literacy components. Stay in this classroom during the entire literacy block (shared reading, spelling/phonics, guided reading, assisted writing, literacy corners). Use techniques of modeling, coaching, scaffolding, and fading to promote the teacher's knowledge and skill in implementing all literacy components. (The following day, rotate to the next model classroom and repeat the same process.)

10:45–11:00   ***Reflection Log:*** Record notes from morning observations in reflection log.

11:00–11:30   ***Lunch***

11:30–11:50   ***Planning Time:*** Plan for working with teachers, prepare for literacy team meeting, and work on assessment data. Plan for teaching children.

11:50–12:30   ***Teaching Children:*** Teach a small group of students (K–3) to promote professional growth in specific literacy areas (guided reading, interactive writing, literature discussion groups, writing-aloud).

12:30–1:15   ***Writers' Workshop in Model Classrooms:*** Return to first-grade model classroom and continue sustained coaching during writers' workshop. Provide adjustable scaffolds for teacher, including demonstrations of mini-lessons followed by teaching observations at another time.

1:15–2:30   ***Working with Other Teachers:*** Demonstrate one literacy component to K–3 teachers who are not receiving sustained coaching. Keep documentation of lesson demonstrations, schedule teaching observations, and provide feedback to teachers.

2:30–3:30   ***Reflecting and Planning:*** Reflect in observation log to document and summarize key learning experiences and observations. Network with other literacy coaches in Arkansas through the Litcoach listserv. Work on details for literacy team meetings.

3:30–4:30   ***Literacy Team Meeting (Tuesdays):*** Share specific information on literacy components with teachers. Coach teachers to use reading and writing data to guide instructional decisions for students. Incorporate the assessment wall into all team meetings. Use colleagues' videotaped lessons to stimulate problem-solving discussions in guided reading and writers' workshop.

Shaping Literate Minds: Developing Self-Regulated Learners by Linda J. Dorm and Carla Soffos. Copyright © 2001. Stenhouse Publishers

Literacy Coach Schedule for Second Year

This schedule is organized to provide sustained coaching in two second-grade classrooms with the goal of developing second-grade model learning labs. The coach will support each model teacher during the entire literacy block at least two days each week for a full year. The following year, these model teachers will become mentor teachers for other second-grade teachers. In the afternoon, the coach will work with K–3 teachers each day for one hour and will teach a small group of students for thirty minutes daily. The coach will also meet with the first-grade mentor teachers as they provide support for the novice first-grade teachers.

7:45–8:00	**Preparation:** Gather materials to coach in one second-grade model classroom, then repeat the same schedule the next day in the other model classroom.
8:00–8:20	**Independent Reading:** Observe second-grade model teacher and students during independent reading. Take at least one running record of a student's reading. Record notes for sharing with the teacher during a later conference.
8:20–11:15	**Sustained Coaching in Model Classroom:** Use the coaching design to support the second-grade teacher in implementing all literacy components. Stay in this classroom during the entire literacy block (strategy-based mini-lessons, spelling/word study, small-group reading, writers' workshop). Use techniques of modeling, coaching, scaffolding, and fading to promote the teacher's knowledge and skill in implementing all literacy components. (The following day, rotate to the next second-grade model classroom and repeat the same process.)
11:15–11:30	**Reflection Log:** Record notes from morning observations in reflection log.
11:30–12:00	**Lunch**
12:00–12:35	**Teaching Children:** Teach a small group of students (K–3) to promote professional growth in specific literacy areas (guided reading, interactive writing, literature discussion groups, writing-aloud).
12:35–1:40	**Writers' Workshop in Model Classrooms:** Return to second-grade model classroom and continue sustained coaching during writers' workshop. Provide adjustable scaffolds for teacher, including demonstrations of mini-lessons followed by teaching observations at another time.
1:40–2:20	**Working with Other Teachers:** Demonstrate one literacy component to K–3 teachers who are not receiving sustained coaching. Keep documentation of lesson demonstrations, schedule teaching observations, and provide feedback to teachers. Observe and support first-grade mentor teachers in working with novice teachers.
2:20–3:20	**Reflecting and Planning:** Reflect in observation log to document and summarize key learning experiences and observations. Network with other literacy coaches in Arkansas through the Litcoach listserv. Work on details for literacy team meetings.
3:30–4:30	**Literacy Team Meeting (Tuesdays):** Share specific information on literacy components with teachers. Coach teachers to use reading and writing data to guide instructional decisions for students. Incorporate the assessment wall into all team meetings. Use colleagues' videotaped lessons to stimulate problem-solving discussions in guided reading and writers' workshop.

Print-Sound Knowledge at the Emergent Level

Reading System	Orthographic System	Writing System
Attends to print using some known letters.	Analyzes letter features; identifies letters based on discriminating features.	Writes known letters with correct formation.
Points to words in a one-to-one match throughout one to three lines of patterned text.	Knows concept of word; constructs single-syllable words in left-to-right order.	Uses spaces between words with greater accuracy.
Recognizes link between known letters and related sounds; articulates first letter in unknown word.	Builds familiar words using slow articulation and direct letter-sound match in single-syllable words.	Recognizes link between known sounds and related letters; slowly articulates word with blended sounds.
Uses a special key word from ABC chart or letter book to help with solving unknown words.	Notices relationship between known letters and sounds as they relate to special key words.	Uses ABC chart and letter books as resources for sound-letter links.
Fluently reads some high-frequency words in easy texts; begins to acquire a reading vocabulary of about twenty frequently encountered words.	Constructs high-frequency words in left-to-right order; says word slowly and coordinates letter-sound match.	Writes a few high-frequency words with accuracy; begins to acquire a writing vocabulary that reflects attention to print during reading.
Self-monitors using high-frequency words and other known visual cues; rereads to cross-check first letter against meaning and structure cues.	Compares and categorizes words by initial sounds and basic rhyming patterns.	Uses first part of known words to help write parts of an unknown word.
Notices unknown words and guesses at the meaning from pictures or how the words are used in text.	Sorts words according to meaning classifications; expands word knowledge by noting meaningful relationships.	Includes new words from reading experiences in writing of texts.

Shaping Literate Minds: Developing Self-Regulated Learners by Linda J. Dorn and Carla Soffos. Copyright © 2001. Stenhouse Publishers

Print-Sound Knowledge at the Early Level

Reading System	Orthographic System	Writing System
Self-monitors reading with greater ease; uses known words and patterns to check on reading; notices words within words; begins to acquire a reading vocabulary of about 150 words from easy and familiar texts.	Spells most unknown words phonetically, including embedded sounds in two- or three-syllable words; later, moves into transitional spelling, noticing common patterns from reading and writing; letter knowledge fast and automatic.	Begins to notice common misspellings in writing and searches through a simple dictionary for corrections; uses resources and checklists; acquires a writing vocabulary that reflects reading experience.
Searches through words in a left-to-right sequence; blends letters into sounds; repeats word as if to confirm identity.	Knows that letters come together in a left-to-right sequence; says words slowly to match letters to sounds; acquires knowledge of interletter relationships from building familiar words (*sh/she; th/the*).	Analyzes sequence of sounds and records corresponding letters; segments and blends sounds in words with increasing ease.
Takes words apart at the larger unit of analysis (consonant digraphs, inflectional endings, onset and rime patterns, blends).	Notices relationship between letter patterns and clusters of sounds; uses known words as a base for adding inflections.	Constructs words using larger units of sound-to-letter patterns; faster and more efficient at writing words.
Reads high-frequency words fast, fluently, and automatically.	Uses known patterns (onset and rime) to build unknown words.	Applies knowledge of onset and rime patterns for writing unknown words.
Becomes faster at noticing errors and initiates multiple attempts to self-correct.	Manipulates letters to form simple analogies.	Notices similarities between word patterns (*mother, father, over*).

Print-Sound Knowledge at the Transitional Level

Reading System	Orthographic System	Writing System
Expands reading vocabulary; shows interest in unfamiliar words that are read to them.	Analyzes unknown words with greater efficiency and speed.	Expands writing vocabulary; includes new and unusual words.
Solves multisyllabic words by noticing parts within the words.	Uses syllable breaks to spell longer words.	Attends to syllables when writing words.
Quickly takes words apart on the run while reading.	Uses more complex analogies to analyze words.	Problem-solves with greater ease and fluency.
Reads longer texts with greater accuracy and fluency.	Analyzes parts of words (inflectional endings, rimes, contractions).	Writes increasingly longer texts with greater accuracy and speed.
Uses word meanings to solve word problems (prefixes, suffixes, roots, compound parts).	Classifies words according to meaningful parts.	Shows flexibility with word choice; tries out different ways of saying a message with the same meaning; revises word choices in writing process; uses a thesaurus as a resource.
Preprocesses error before making a mistake.	Spells words with greater accuracy; shows evidence of transitional spelling of words with more unusual patterns.	Uses dictionaries, editing checklists, and other resources to self-correct writing.

Shaping Literate Minds: Developing Self-Regulated Learners by Linda J. Dorn and Carla Soffos. Copyright © 2001. Stenhouse Publishers

Print-Sound Knowledge at the Fluent Level

Reading System	Orthographic System	Writing System
Has an extensive reading vocabulary; reads longer texts with specialized content and unusual words; learns new words daily.	Has flexible control of spelling patterns; knows when words do not look right; can spell most words with minimal attention.	Has an extensive writing vocabulary; writes longer texts with good word choices; uses new words from reading.
Applies knowledge of word meaning to reading texts with more complex language structures.	Classifies words according to word meanings, including figurative and descriptive language.	Uses figurative language (similes, metaphors) and descriptive phrases to enhance message.
Responds to reading at many different levels; applies knowledge about word meanings across different texts; makes predictions about word meanings and checks within texts; refines word knowledge.	Notices multiple meanings of words; acquires a mental dictionary of word meanings.	Uses a range of resources, including thesaurus, dictionary, encyclopedia, and other research materials to plan and inform writing.

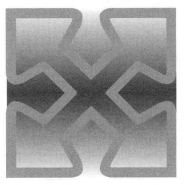

References

Balkman, J. A. 2001. "Accelerated Change in Reading Instruction: The Arkansas Comprehensive School Reform Model." *Journal of School Improvement* (May). Tempe, AZ: North Central Association Commission on Schools.

Bransford, J., A. Brown, and R. Cocking, eds. 1999. *How People Learn: Brain, Mind, Experience, and School.* National Research Council. Washington, DC: National Academy Press.

Bruner, J. 1966. *Toward a Theory of Instruction.* Cambridge, MA: Harvard University Press.

———. 1990. *Acts of Meaning.* Cambridge, MA: Harvard University Press.

Campione, J., A. Shapiro, and A. Brown. 1995. "Forms of Transfer in a Community of Learners: Flexible Learning and Understanding." In A. McKeough, J. Lupart, and A. Marini, eds., *Teaching for Transfer: Fostering Generalization in Learning.* Hillsdale, NJ: Lawrence Erlbaum.

Cazden, C. B. 1988. *Classroom Discourse: The Language of Teaching and Learning.* Portsmouth, NH: Heinemann.

Clay, M. 1991. *Becoming Literate: The Construction of Inner Control.* Portsmouth, NH: Heinemann.

———. 1993. *An Observation Survey of Early Literacy Achievement.* Portsmouth, NH: Heinemann.

———. 1998. *By Different Paths to Common Outcomes.* Portland, ME: Stenhouse.

Collins, A., J. S. Brown, and A. Holum. 1991. "Cognitive Apprenticeship: Making Thinking Visible." *American Educator* 6 (11): 38–46.

Collins, A., J. S. Brown, and S. E. Newman. 1989. "Cognitive Apprenticeship: Teaching the Crafts of Reading, Writing, and Mathematics." In L. B. Resnick, ed., *Knowing, Learning and Instruction: Essays in Honor of Robert Glazer.* Hillsdale, NJ: Lawrence Erlbaum.

Dewey, J. 1998. *How We Think.* Boston: Houghton Mifflin Company. Originally published in 1910.

Diaz, R., C. Neal, and M. Amaya-Williams. 1990. "The Social Origins of Self-Regulation." In L. Moll, ed., *Vygotsky and Education: Instructional Implications and Applications of Sociohistorical Psychology.* Cambridge: Cambridge University Press.

Donaldson, M. 1978. *Children's Minds.* London: Fontana.

Dorn, L. 1997. The Development of Self-Regulation in Reading. Unpublished paper, University of Arkansas at Little Rock.

———. 1999. *Organizing for Literacy: Four Inservice Videotapes.* Portland, ME: Stenhouse.

Dorn, L., C. French, and T. Jones. 1998. *Apprenticeship in Literacy: Transitions Across Reading and Writing.* Portland, ME: Stenhouse.

Dorn, L. and C. Soffos. 2001a. *Literacy Task Cards. Inservice Videotape.* San Diego: Teaching Resource Center.

———. 2001b. *Scaffolding Young Writers: A Writers' Workshop Approach.* Portland, ME: Stenhouse.

———. 2001c. *Spelling Inservice Videotape.* San Diego: Teaching Resource Center.

Dorn, L., C. Soffos, and T. Treat. 2001. *Literacy Task Cards.* San Diego: Teaching Resource Center.

Dorn, L., and D. Williams. 2000. The Arkansas Comprehensive Early Literacy Model for School Change. Unpublished report, University of Arkansas at Little Rock.

Eisner, E. 1998. *The Kind of Schools We Need.* Portsmouth, NH: Heinemann.

Fountas, I., and G. S. Pinnell. 1996. *Guided Reading: Good First Teaching for All Children.* Portsmouth, NH: Heinemann.

———. 1999. *Matching Books to Readers: Using Leveled Books in Guided Reading K–3.* Portsmouth, NH: Heinemann.

Gentry, R., and J. W. Gillet. 1993. *Teaching Kids to Spell.* Portsmouth, NH: Heinemann.

Hogan, K., and M. Pressley. 1997. *Scaffolding Student Learning: Instructional Approaches and Issues.* Cambridge, MA: Brookline Books.

Jorgenson, L. 1999. A Study of Teacher/Child Intersubjectivity: Co-Constructing Meaning Through Conversation. Unpublished paper, University of Arkansas at Little Rock.

Keene, C. 1998. *The Hidden Treasures.* Old Tappan, NJ: Simon and Schuster.

Kerbow, D. J., J. Gwynne, and B. Jacob. 1999. Evaluation of Achievement Gains at the Primary Level. Paper presented at American Educational Research Association Meeting, Montreal, Canada, April.

Lupart, J. 1996. "Exceptional Learners and Teaching for Transfer." In A. McKeough, J. Lupart, and A. Marini, eds., *Teaching for Transfer: Fostering Generalization in Learning.* Hillsdale, NJ: Lawrence Erlbaum.

Mercer, N. 1995. *The Guided Construction of Knowledge: Talk Amongst Teachers and Learners.* Bristol, PA: Multilingual Matters.

New Standards Primary Committee. 1999. *Reading and Writing Grade by Grade: Primary Literacy Standards for Kindergarten Through Third Grade.* Washington, DC: National Center on Education and the Economy and the University of Pittsburgh.

Pinnell, G. S., and I. C. Fountas. 1998. *Word Matters: Teaching Phonics and Spelling in the Reading/Writing Classroom.* Portsmouth, NH: Heinemann.

Randell, B. 1994. *Mushrooms for Dinner.* Crystal Lake, IL: Rigby.

Randell, B., J. Giles, and A. Smith. 1996. *At the Zoo.* Crystal Lake, IL: Rigby.

Reading Unlimited. 1976. *The Missing Necklace.* Glenview, IL: Scott Foresman.

Rogoff, B. 1990. *Apprenticeship in Thinking: Cognitive Development in Social Context.* New York: Oxford University Press.

Rothman, R. 1996. *Organizing So All Children Can Learn: Applying the Principles of Learning.* Washington, DC: National Center on Education and the Economy.

Sharmat, M. W., and R. Weinman. 1993. *Nate the Great and the Pillowcase.* New York: Bantam Doubleday Dell.

Slobodkina, E. 1987. *Caps for Sale.* New York: HarperCollins. Originally published in 1940.

Smith, A. 1996. *Looking Down.* Crystal Lake, IL: Rigby.

Snowball, D., and F. Bolton. 1999. *Spelling K–8: Planning and Teaching.* Portland, ME: Stenhouse.

Vygotsky, L., M. Cole, V. John-Steiner, S. Scribner, and E. Souberman. 1978. *Mind in Society: The Development of Higher Psychological Processes.* Cambridge, MA: Harvard University Press.

Ward, C. 1988. *Cookie's Week.* New York: G. P. Putnam's Sons.

Wertsch, J. V., ed. 1985. *Culture, Communication, and Cognition: Vygotskian Perspectives.* Cambridge: Cambridge University Press.

Wood, D. 1998. *How Children Think and Learn.* 2d ed. Malden, MA: Blackwell.

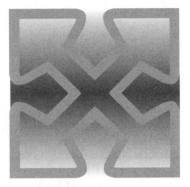

Index

Other Stenhouse Books and Inservice Videotapes by Linda J. Dorn

Scaffolding Young Writers
A Writers' Workshop Approach

Linda J. Dorn and Carla Soffos

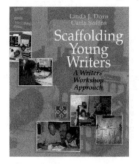

The goal of teaching writing is to create independent and self-motivated writers. When students write more often, they become better at writing. They acquire habits, skills, and strategies that enable them to learn more about the craft of writing. Yet they require the guidance and support of a more knowledgeable person who understands the writing process, the changes over time in writing development, and specific techniques and procedures for teaching writing.

Adopting an apprenticeship approach, the authors show how explicit teaching, good models, clear demonstrations, established routines, assisted teaching followed by independent practice, and self-regulated learning are all fundamental in establishing a successful writers' workshop. There is a detailed chapter on organizing for writers' workshop, including materials, components, routines, and procedures. Other chapters provide explicit guidelines for designing productive mini-lessons and student conferences.

Scaffolding Young Writers also features:

- an overview of how children become writers;
- analyses of students' samples according to informal and formal writing assessments;
- writing checklists, benchmark behaviors, and rubrics based on national standards;
- examples of teaching interactions during mini-lessons and writing conferences;
- illustrations of completed forms and checklists with detailed descriptions, and blank reproducible forms in the appendix for classroom use.

Instruction is linked with assessment throughout the book, so that all teaching interactions are grounded in what children already know and what they need to know as they develop into independent writers.

Apprenticeship in Literacy
Transitions Across Reading and Writing

Linda J. Dorn, Cathy French, and Tammy Jones

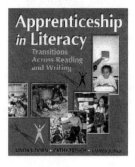

This easy-to-read text will guide K–3 teachers as they develop a reading and writing program for all their students. An apprenticeship approach to literacy emphasizes the role of the teacher in providing demonstrations, engaging children, monitoring their understanding, providing timely support and, ultimately, withdrawing that support as the child gains independence.

Drawing on authentic classroom examples—student writing samples, class schedules, photographs, and rich transcriptions of teaching and learning interactions—the authors illustrate instruction that is aimed at children's learning zones. As children become more competent readers and writers, the instructional interactions are adjusted to accommodate their higher-level learning.

Here is a wealth of in-depth information, specific strategies, and organizational formats in literacy areas such as:

- principles of apprenticeship literacy;
- learning to read from a cognitive apprenticeship approach, including the roles of read-aloud, familiar reading, and shared reading;
- guided reading, including flexible grouping, reading and writing links, and instructional interactions that emphasize problem-solving strategies;
- helping children develop writing strategies through interactive writing, writing aloud, and revising and editing transactions;
- transitions in children's independent writing, including their relationship to modeling and coaching demonstrations during assisted writing;
- helping children acquire phonological knowledge, including activities that guide children in manipulating letters, sounds, and spelling patterns;
- a typical day of putting it all together in two apprenticeship settings: Angela's first-grade classroom and Carla's Title I reading program;

- using school-based professional literacy teams to support teachers in developing an effective literacy program for their children.

No detail is lost. The authors also cover such practical matters as establishing routines and organizing the classroom environment, including rotation schedules for meeting with small groups of children, lists of materials for establishing literacy corners, and literacy corner activities designed to provide the children with opportunities for independent practice.

Organizing for Literacy
Four Inservice Videotapes

Linda J. Dorn

These programs are designed to support classroom teachers as they implement a balanced literacy program that applies the principles of apprenticeship theory. The tapes illustrate the reciprocal nature of teaching and learning across a range of reading and writing events. The study guide included in the set provides focus questions for viewing teacher/student interactions and for analyzing the children's reading and writing behaviors over the four tapes.

Organizing the Classroom
The classroom segments on this tape illustrate the importance of a well-organized environment that includes opportunities for children to work in their assisted and independent learning zones. We invite you into Theresa's classroom to observe how she provides her first grade students with a balanced literacy program that includes small and large group instruction and opportunities to work independently in well-designed literacy corners.

Learning About Reading
Children learn about reading through a range of literacy experiences that include familiar reading, shared reading, reading aloud, and guided reading. As they engage in problem-solving interactions with a more knowledgeable person, children apply flexible strategies for learning how to read. In the video, you will see how Theresa and Carla provide their first graders with opportunities to read in whole group and small group interactions.

Learning About Writing
The reciprocal nature of reading and writing is emphasized in a balanced literacy program. On the video, you will observe the same children from their guided reading groups as they work in their assisted writing groups. Theresa and Carla provide a range of writing opportunities that are specially designed to scaffold children toward independence in writing.

Learning About Words
As children read and write, they acquire important knowledge and strategies for problem-solving on words. During shared reading, poetry is used to direct children's attention to word patterns; and during reading aloud, stories are used to help children learn about the expressive qualities of words. In literacy corners, children apply their knowledge about words in specially designed activities that are based on their reading and writing accomplishments. Writing is embedded in all word building activities, including the use of writing vocabulary notebooks, structural analysis notebooks, student dictionaries, and personal thesauruses.

A detailed viewing guide accompanies this set of tapes.